Ornamental Alphabets and Initials

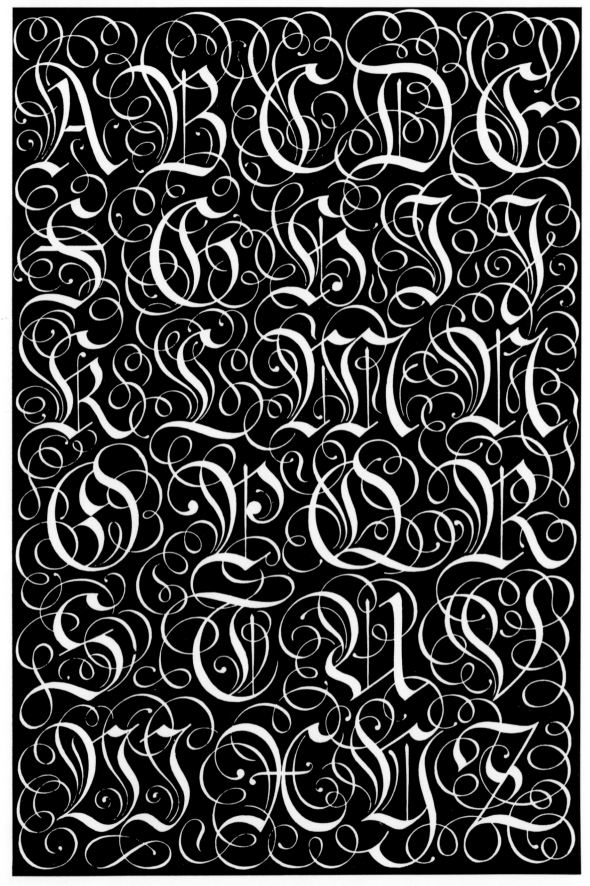

Wood-engraved German Fraktur alphabet by Leo Wyatt, *c.*1970

Ornamental Alphabets and Initials

Alison Harding

With 142 illustrations, 14 in colour

THAMES AND HUDSON

To A.S.F.

Printed and bound in Japan by Dai Nippon

Introduction

THE PURPOSE of bringing together this collection of alphabets and initials is twofold. Firstly, I hope that it may show some part of the extraordinary diversity of creative impulse that, through the centuries, has been applied to that most familiar of forms, the letter. Secondly, by tracing some of the influences that have inspired or directed the designers and decorators of letters, I hope to extend understanding of the way in which this particular aspect of artistic endeavour has survived so many changes of fashion and technological innovations. From the wide range of material available – much of it already familiar and some little known – selection has inevitably been difficult. My choices, whether of a single initial or of a complete alphabet, have their only real justification in the conviction expressed by Joan Evans in *Style in Ornament*, that 'they will have achieved their end if they make the reader look at the infinitely varied patterns of the man-created world of ornament with a new intentness'.

The material presented in this book falls into three main historical groups, which correspond roughly to the medieval, Renaissance up to early Victorian, and modern periods. Although the first is dominated by the manuscript letter, the emphasis here is upon the way in which certain decorative elements and uses of the letter are carried over into early printing, and upon the emergence of early alphabet books. In the second group, the pre-eminence of the classical letter is shown alongside the continuation of calligraphy as an art, and the further development of pictorial alphabet books. The third group, from about 1810 onward, shows the effects of technical advances upon the design and use of all kinds of decorative letter, the influence of alphabet collections, and the contributions of some individual artists to the development of alphabet design. Though these divisions are necessarily arbitrary, they do reflect important changes of emphasis in the history of the book in Europe – for example, the changeover from manuscript to printed book in the fifteenth century – and, in particular, they indicate increasing complexity in the relationship between individual creativity on the one hand, and mechanical production on the other.

However, it will be seen from the initials and alphabets themselves that, in spite of significant changes in technique or attitude, there are in some respects surprising elements of continuity from one phase to the next. Particular ideas or motifs tend to recur, often moving from one country to another within a remarkably short time. The letter A is frequently presented as a draughtsman's compass or dividers, from medieval times through to the present day; a variety of styles show letters composed of twigs, branches, or even whole trees; and letters decorated with highly organized scrolls, tendrils, leaves and flowers have been typical of each return to classical styles of ornamentation. Such recurring themes – whether or not they are part of a conscious archaism or revival – represent decorative traditions from which there have been some spectacular departures: for example, in late eighteenth-century Germany, a complete alphabet is formed of architectural plans; and one twentieth-century alphabet is inspired by the shapes of seaweeds. Yet even such apparent aberrations may be seen as part of a larger pattern of ideas affecting letter design, for the connection between letter forms and architecture is one of which the Renaissance theorists were fully aware, and the search for new inspiration from natural shapes may be traced in the naturalistic decoration of letters in some medieval manuscripts.

Ornamented letters, whether produced as single initials or as complete alphabets, seem to have developed in two distinct, though interrelated, directions. There is the primarily functional letter, which, though decorative, serves as a pointer in a text, as part of a line of titling, or as a means of information on a poster or advertising display. And there is the purely creative letter, which may appear unrelated to a text, being composed of elements chosen by the artist and perhaps achieving the status of a work of art in its own right. In some periods, the functional and the creative overlap – notably in medieval manuscripts where the text is often familiar and the artist, though anonymous, can create an initial containing patterns or images that have as much impact as the written word. An even earlier example, the Book of Kells, contains some pages dominated by complex initials whose impact is entirely visual, and others where lesser initials are used to complement the text. In the 'grotesque' alphabets, the image is more important than the actual letter, which serves simply as a framework for Gothic fantasy, demanding an imaginative response from the observer rather than communicating a verbal message. At another period, as in the first half of the twentieth century in Great Britain, the demands of clarity and legibility may be regarded as paramount, and any ornament on a printed page must serve a typographic purpose.

But whether one looks at a decorative letter in relation to a page or at an alphabet created as a picture book for instruction or pleasure, one is constantly aware that in spite of its imaginative scope the art of letter design has to be based upon a formal discipline. The shape of each character dictates its identity, challenging the artist to clothe it in such a way that, though it may convey a new message, it remains familiar. The artist appears sometimes to have been sidetracked from his main purpose by his own inventiveness – the picture takes over and the letter is hardly discernible. Sometimes the conventions of an age or the use of a new technique prove to be more significant factors than the personality of the artist, and a letter may be technically accomplished, but little more. In other examples, the balance between technical skill and the communication of ideas or images is successfully achieved, resulting in memorable, or even unique, characters. Whether the designer is himself chiefly preoccupied with the purity of his chosen letterform, or whether he prefers to exploit it in order to indulge his own flights of fancy, it is clear that the claims of function and ornamentation may not always be easily reconciled.

The decorated letters of hand-produced manuscripts seem to have fulfilled a purpose that was both practical and aesthetic. They reinforced the instructional or religious message with patterns of varying complexity and style, or with images tending toward fantasy or reality according to whim or convention. But it does appear that where Romanesque influence prevails, the artist has considerably greater scope for treating letters in an imaginative way – turning them into animal or bird shapes which are allowed to move without the constriction of letterforms – than is allowed by the more austere Carolingian style, with its less personal emphasis upon pattern and line. By the time designs for decorated alphabets and single initials begin to appear in the pattern books used by artists from the late twelfth century onward, the movement towards naturalism and the separation of the functions of scribe and artist are adding impetus to the expression of individuality. Little is known about the early pattern books, which may have been intended for the use of carvers or masons as well as for scribes and illuminators; their style varies from the stylized birds and beasts and formal interlacing of the Cambridge pattern book to the freely developed flower-and-leaf decorations in a fifteenth-century sketchbook for the guidance of illuminators. Originally they seem to have been compiled chiefly to provide models for the practitioners of decorated letters; only later do they become demonstrations of the skill and inventiveness of individual artists. Although the 'Bergamo' alphabet clearly inspired imitators from other parts of Europe, including England and the Low Countries, it is not slavishly copied – a new artist often adds an extra detail or exploits the Gothic letterform in a different way. In the original alphabet the framework of the letter is clear; in the fifteenth-century version by the master 'E.S.' it is discernible through little else than the different angles of birds' wings.

By this time, it is evident that the letter has reached an extreme of Gothicism in which the form has all but disappeared. Communication is through images, unsupported by a text, and chosen by the artist. The question of a letter's form, together with its function as a means of communicating verbal rather than visual messages, has become the province of the printer or typecutter. So the unity of purpose shown in early manuscript books, which has already been fragmented to a certain extent by the separation of the individual skills that contributed to their production, is now superseded by the differing purposes of the mechanically printed book on the one hand, and personal creativity on the other. The invention of movable type and the development of the art of engraving both on wood and on metal mean that a major art form – that of the hand-produced book with its magnificent illuminated initials and smaller decorated letters – recedes into the background.

This is not to decry the achievements of the printers, engravers and letter-designers of the early Renaissance. They mastered the new skills with incredible speed, so that according to one estimation 'nearly 9,000,000 copies of books were already in circulation by the end of the fifteenth century'. But this same efficiency and speed had a number of crucial effects upon the design and usage of initial letters. In the early days of printing it was natural enough for the printer to follow the example of the scribe by using historiated and other decorative letters in 'block books', which were closely modelled upon manuscript books. But whereas the complex, often almost illegible, illuminated letter was usually part of a familiar word – the I of Incipit or the B of Beatus, for example – the printed initial came with increasing frequency to be part of unfamiliar matter. The need for ease of understanding as well as for more efficient production must have contributed to both the reduction in size of initial letters and the simplification of their design. Initially hand-drawn in spaces left by the printer, they were later engraved on wood or metal and inserted into their place in the text as separate blocks; these circumscribed the decoration within a square or rectangular shape, sometimes enclosed within a single or double line. The artist of such letters had to be, *faute de mieux*, a miniaturist. Then, however great his skill or originality, his creation was rapidly dispersed and repeated, perhaps ending up in texts for which it was not intended, perhaps debased in a version produced by a different printer, or simply printed so many times from the original block that it lost its freshness and relevance. So while the printer succeeded in solving the practical problems of integrating text and ornament, the creativity evident in early mechanical book production began to be channelled away from historiated and animated letters towards more formal and timeless designs, appropriate for a wider variety of printed text.

The replacement of the Gothic letter by classical letterforms can be seen in part as a result of the rapid communication of ideas made possible by the development of printing. Towards the end of the fifteenth century, Ratdolt was producing in Venice blocks of gracious letters surrounded by delicate yet sinewy decoration, in direct contrast to the Gothic letter which often overflows into the surrounding decoration or, as in the Bergamo alphabet, provides no more than a frame for a design. The happy coexistence of classical and Gothic letters – both giving rise to decorations ranging from the historiated to simple flower-and-leaf motifs – lasted for a comparatively short period. As grotesque letters become increasingly the province of the calligrapher and engraver, the printer and type designer seem chiefly preoccupied with the letterform, and this, of course, affects the decorated initial as well as the alphabet book. The latter is used more and more by calligraphers as the means of expressing, and putting into practice, their theories of letter design. It is to their art rather than to the printed book that one looks for the survival of the elements of Gothic fantasy and personal creativity. The aesthetic problem of the place of ornamentation in printing has remained unresolved to the present time; in the sixteenth century it reflects the continuation of the Renaissance attitude towards artistic matters of all kinds. The search for the perfect number, the ideal shape, and the correct relationship between human endeavour and abstract principle exerted so strong an influence over printers and letter designers that, from the disorderly, almost frantic, proliferation of ornamented letters in early printed books, only a few designs survived.

One of the most influential theorists, Geofroy Tory, was also a designer, and his *Champ Fleury* of 1529 provides a useful guide to the alphabets of his time. As well as presenting his famous 'Attic' letters, which were to dominate future type design and were related by Tory to mathematical principles and to the proportions of the human body, he illustrated a floriated alphabet which was to influence the decorative initial in European printing over the next two centuries.

Woodcut letter with 'lily-of-the-valley' motif, Augsburg *c.*1480

At the opposite end of the spectrum from his classical letters, he showed a 'fantastic' alphabet, originating, he claimed, in Egyptian hieroglyphs, 'being made from symbols and pictures'. This kind of alphabet may have had some occult significance, but the fact that Tory regards these letters as important is interesting in the light of their re-emergence, after a period of obscurity, in modern surreal or symbolic alphabets. The association of letters with the objects is also an important element in early instructional or children's alphabet books, but here the letter is used alongside the image, rather than being replaced by it. Among Tory's alphabets there is also a description of the 'cadeaulx . . . used at the beginning of books written by hand'; these letters, 'which the teachers of writing embellished and enriched . . . with foliage, faces, birds and a thousand pretty things', may be regarded as survivors from the medieval styles of letter decoration. Though popular at first in printed books, they became, as Tory states, confined to the calligrapher's art, which often developed them to a high degree of sophistication.

It is indeed to the great writing-books that one must turn to find a continuation of the exploitation of the letter as an image, or the use of its shape as the starting-point for inventive elaboration. Here are the birds, beasts and human figures that inhabit the Gothic alphabets, as well as the *litterae florissae* indulged in by the later medieval scribe. These are the delicate traceries that often accompanied secondary initials, their tendrils reaching into the border of the manuscript and not, like the formal leaves and flowers of Tory's floriated letters, confined within a regular shape. The earlier pen-work initials, like those of later calligraphers, are, however, only at first glance to be taken as mere random extravaganzas; their construction was, in fact, an organized art, and recognized as such in the 'hierarchies of decoration' belonging to the production of later manuscripts. The construction of flourished capitals and complex borders in writing-books is essentially a discipline, but a creative one, despite the fact that the books of Neudorffer in Germany, Arrighi and Tagliente in Italy, and Juan d'Yciar in Spain were widely copied in the sixteenth century, being reproduced by wood or copper engraving. Among the alphabets of Juan d'Yciar is one of Gothic letters decorated with a variety of intricate patterns, and it was of course through the work of writing-masters that the Gothic hands were chiefly preserved. During the seventeenth century, English calligraphers came to the fore, in particular John Ayres and William Elder, who were followed by George Bickham. Bickham's *Universal Penman* made an important contribution to the art of engraving, which, as it developed, was used in the production of some fine alphabet books. In these the heavy baroque ornament gradually gives way to a stronger pictorial element; delicately drawn and more naturalistic birds, flowers and animals join the classical figures typical of rococo style so that, once again, towards the end of the eighteenth century, the letter becomes less important than the picture associated with it.

In printed books, the function of the initial letter had remained virtually unchanged. In the long term, the achievement of Renaissance letter designers seems to have had an adverse effect upon printed decorative letters, though no doubt political upheavals and the restrictive forces of Reformation morality also

Initials from the writing book *Arte Subtilissima* by Juan d'Yciar, Saragossa 1550

9

contributed to the apparent dearth of inspiration, as well as to the dramatic reduction in the number of initial letters used. Yet in Holland, some decorative letters in the seventeenth century were of a high quality; Dutch artists and engravers came to be much in demand in England but it was not until the end of the seventeenth century, when printing restrictions were lifted, that the way was open for English printing to develop once again to a high standard. Meanwhile, the 'factotum' or 'passe-partout' initial was much in evidence; this consisted of an engraved block into which a letter could be inserted according to the printer's need. Though this kind of letter may be regarded as an unimaginative solution, it had at least the merit of providing a minimum standard of decoration, and some factotums were engraved skilfully. More interesting are the many variations of the 'flowerpot' or 'urn' designs which appeared particularly in the Low Countries; their detail and often bold lines are reminiscent of the woodcut floral decorations of early printing. Travel scenes, architectural detail, and sometimes science or natural history are themes that gradually appear in the background of some initials. To match the skills of the engravers, an increasing command of line and perspective are apparent on the artists' part, especially in Italian initials, in which, in the eighteenth century, the letterform also begins to acquire a new boldness.

Engraved 'factotum' initial, English, late 17th century

A gradual resurgence of creativity can be detected in some of the elaborate engraved title-pages of the period, which display different kinds of decorative letters, some with complex flourishes, others with patterned infilling. The interrelation of calligraphy and printing is also evident in engraved trade cards, which are often highly decorative; but the writing-book has lost much of its momentum, and calligraphy remains overshadowed by printing until the 'modern Renaissance' of the early twentieth century in Great Britain and Germany. Alphabet books, like other picture books of the time, begin to reflect an increasing interest in natural forms. In an Italian alphabet book, for example, ruins and mountains are part of a landscape background to letters made from pine trees, a conception closer in spirit to the grotesque alphabets of the fifteenth century than to the classical letters of the Italian Renaissance. But a preoccupation with form is still all-important in the majority of late eighteenth-century typographic productions. Though Ibarra in Spain and Fournier in France both used charming capital letters with flourished decorations, these were models of restraint, and even their more elaborate initials, composed of fleurons (printers' flowers), appeared formal. In England the newly emergent Caslon foundry produced some fine initials in the seventeenth-century style, but it was not until the development of the Victorian 'fat faces', in wooden letters with engraved designs and in metal-cast ornamental types, that English printing broke away from classical severity, and ornament of all kinds took on a new exuberance.

It is to the nineteenth century then that we owe not only the rapid exploitation of reprographic processes and the use of colour in printing, but also the creative energy and receptivity needed for letter design to shake off the inhibitions imposed by the demands of the Renaissance theorists. Initials of all kinds came into their own again, in areas ranging from commercial advertising to elaborate, illuminated gift books. Thomas Astle's *The Origin and Progress of Writing* was only one of several scholarly works to stimulate the growth of renewed interest in

Formation of the letter S, from Edward Cocker's *Magnum in Parvo; or, the Pens Perfection*, London 1672

the decorative arts of the past. These provided inspiration not only for the art historian in his attempts to achieve near-perfect facsimiles, but also for the alphabet designer in his creation of special effects and for artists, both professional and amateur, in emulating medieval styles of decoration and illumination. The works of Henry Shaw, Owen Jones and Noel Humphreys in England, of Silvestre and Midolle in France, and, later in the century, of Petzendorfer in Germany, are outstanding both in their use of the newly established techniques of lithographic engraving and in their exploitation of the possibilities of colour in ornament. In their creation of new initials and new alphabets, as well as in their revival of older material, these artists influenced not only the design of books but also the increasing awareness in popular printing of the decorated letter as a means of display in publicity and advertising. Many of the letters used in the Victorian period seem to take on individuality according to their decorative style – some are almost ethereal, with filigree tracery, others robust, three-dimensional and shown casting heavy shadows. As far as form and legibility are concerned, they may fail the tests of the purists; but they represent a disregard for convention and for restrictiveness that, in this nineteenth-century context, is, initially at least, healthy and productive. Though, as Nicolete Gray states, 'the Victorian approach was too antiquarian to produce much that was really original', it can, nevertheless, be seen as an important preparation 'for art nouveau designers [who] thus inherited a gothic way of thinking from which we have been completely cut off by the ruthless exclusiveness of the Trajan lettering revival of the beginning of this century.'

This description sums up much that has occurred during the hundred years since the beginnings of the Arts and Crafts Movement, initiated by William Morris and his followers. This movement can be seen as a conscious attempt on the part of designers, artists and craftsmen to raise standards. Now the wood-engraved initial (already revitalized by Victorian illustrators and engravers) acquired, in the designs of Morris and Ricketts, a fresh emphasis upon the shape of the letterform. Whether based on a bold Gothic or a gracious Venetian style, these revivals demonstrated the growing preoccupation with line, which, combined with oriental influences, was reflected in the initials, borders, illustrations and book bindings of the art nouveau period. Though many lettering designs produced at this time were imaginative as well as technically competent, few – among them those of Beardsley and the *Jugendstil* artists Eckmann and Behrens – survived the immediate fashions of what soon came to be regarded as a self-indulgent aesthetic. Soon ornamentation of all kinds gave way to the severity of functionalism, inevitably limiting the creative scope of alphabets and initials. While interest in the letters of the past continued to be strong in France and in the United States, English book design moved closer to that of Germany, for example in the work of the Cranach Press. In the striving for simplicity and modernity that characterized the 'English Renaissance', even the combination of classical letterform with tree-and-leaf decoration shown in the initials created by Pissarro for the Eragny Press was seen in some quarters as exceeding the bounds of purity of line and ornamental restraint upheld by typographers of the 1920s in England.

The chief concern of British artists and designers was to establish traditional styles of letter that would be appropriate for modern mass production. The art of calligraphy developed new impetus under the influence of Edward Johnston and once again had a direct effect upon printing, though this time in the direction of restraint rather than of sixteenth-century 'Gothic imagination'. Eric Gill's judgment, that 'letters are things, not pictures of things', informs his design of initial letters and alphabets. Though in some respects they follow logically upon the heels of the more severe kind of art nouveau letter, they are among the more creative manifestations of the new classicism. Later initials, ranging from the dignity and simplicity of van Krimpen's letters to the more complex boldness of Barnett Freedman's alphabet for the Baynard Press, were still contained within the regular block shape – any escape into the margins of a book remained unthinkable, despite more radical forces that were making themselves felt in book and type design on the continent and in the United States.

Initial letter designed by Jan van Krimpen for the Curwen Press, *c.* 1935

The change, when it came, was one of mood rather than direction. In the post-war years, renewed interest was shown in Victorian styles of letter, which were accepted as an important element in designs for signs and posters for the Festival of Britain in 1951. Meanwhile, on the continent, and particularly in Switzerland, lettering of a more innovative kind could be seen in the designs of Imre Reiner. But the imaginative exploitation of letterforms by creative artists remained the exception rather than the rule: development in alphabet design continued to be geared to the needs of modern book production and mass communication, and conditioned by technical advances such as photoreproduction and transfer lettering. Writing in the 1950s, Laurence Scarfe called the trend towards

Victorian and similar revivals in lettering a 'pastiche typography', which was being used for reasons of nostalgia rather than in any truly creative sense.

Perhaps it is partly because of such restriction of purpose that the modern design and use of alphabets and initials have largely failed to demonstrate the energetic exploration of ideas and flexibility of line necessary to the survival of the letter as an art form. Only in recent years, perhaps generated by the renewed need for visual images and flexible forms, does there seem to have been any positive response to Scarfe's call for newly created letters that reflect the other visual arts of the present day. What is abundantly clear from the examples of past movements affecting the decoration of alphabets and initials, is that the unity of impulse and discipline needed to transform them into minor works of art does not appear as an isolated cultural phenomenon. Perhaps today, with the increasing visual influences of film and television, and the availability of ever more sophisticated methods for reproducing the creative efforts of the graphic artist, letters may again return as important images, containing a mystery and significance that can only be achieved by a combination of the familiar with the outrageous.

Bibliography

LETTER DESIGN AND HISTORY OF ALPHABETS AND LETTERS

Alexander, J.J.G. *The Decorated Letter* London 1978
Biggs, John Reginald *Letter-forms and Lettering: towards an understanding of the shapes of letters* Poole 1977
Diringer, David *The Alphabet: a key to the history of mankind* London 1948
—*The Illuminated Book: Its History and Production* London 1958
Gray, Nicolete *Lettering as Drawing: Contour and Silhouette* London 1970
—*Lettering as Drawing: The Moving Line* London 1970
Haab, Armin and Haetenschweiler, Walter (eds.) *Lettera* vols 1–4 Teufen 1962
Harling, Robert *Alphabet and Image 1946–1948* New York 1975
Johnson, A.F. *Decorative Initial Letters* London 1931
Lehner, Ernst *Alphabets and Ornaments* New York 1952, 1968
McLean, Ruari *Pictorial Alphabets* London 1969
Massin ( ) *Letter and Image* London 1970
Nesbitt, Alexander *Decorative Alphabets and Initials* New York 1959
Plomer, Henry R. *English Printers' Ornament* London 1924
Scarfe, Laurence *Alphabets* London 1954
Tory, Geofroy *Champ Fleury* New York 1967

CALLIGRAPHY

Bonacini, Claudio *Bibliografia delle Arti Scrittorie e della Caligrafia* Florence 1953
Fairbank, Alfred John *A Book of Scripts* Harmondsworth 1949
—, Wolpe B. *Renaissance Handwriting* London 1960
Morison, Stanley (ed.) *Calligraphy: 1535–1885* Milan 1962
Osley, A.S. *Luminario: an introduction to Italian writing books of the sixteenth and seventeenth centuries* Nieuwkoop 1972
Whalley, Joyce Irene and Kaden, Vera C. *The Universal Penman: a survey of western calligraphy from the Roman period to 1980* London 1980

TYPOGRAPHY AND PRINTING – GRAPHIC DESIGN

Clair, Colin *A Chronology of Printing* London 1969
—*A History of European Printing* London 1976
Goldschmidt, Philip *The Printed Book of the Renaissance* Cambridge 1958
Gray, Nicolete *19th Century Ornamented Types and Title Pages* London 1938
Hart, Horace *Notes on a Century of Typography at the University Press, Oxford (1693–1794)* Oxford 1970
Lewis, John N.C. and Brinkley, J. *Graphic Design* London 1954
Morison, Stanley *Four Centuries of Fine Printing* London 1924, 1960
Owens, Leslie Thomas *J.H. Mason 1875–1951, Scholar Printer* London 1976
Updike, Daniel Berkeley *Printing Types, their History, Forms and Use*, 2 vols Cambridge, USA 1922

BOOK DESIGN AND ILLUSTRATION

Hind, Arthur Mayger *An Introduction to a History of Woodcut* 2 vols London 1935, 1963
Holloway, Owen E. *French Rococo Book Illustrations* London 1969

McLean, Ruari *Victorian Book Design and Colour Printing* London 1963
Studio, The *The Art of the Book* London 1914
  —*Modern Book Production* London 1928, 1938
Taylor, John Russell *The Art Nouveau Book in Britain* London 1966

Acknowledgments

I would like to thank the following institutions and individuals for the provision of material and/or assistance

INSTITUTIONS: Bibliothèque Nationale, Paris; Victoria and Albert Museum, London; Bodleian Library, Oxford; Fitzwilliam Museum, Cambridge; St Bride Printing Library, London; Biblioteca Civica, Bergamo; University of Exeter; Exeter College of Art and Design; Devon and Exeter Institution

INDIVIDUALS: Mr M.C. Brand and Mr A.S. Fotheringham (Marlborough Rare Books); Mr Robin de Beaumont; Mr Nicholas Abrams; Mr Mike Nott; Mr Charles Cox; Ms Susan Mosdell; Dr L. Watson (Victoria and Albert Library); Mrs S. Stirling and Mr G.J. Paley (Devon and Exeter Institution Library); Mrs R. Barry (Graphics Library, Exeter College of Art and Design); Mr J. Stirling and Mr M. Myhill (Exeter University Library); Mr James Mosley (St Bride Printing Library); Mr Colin Cuthbert
Mr Tony Mann (for reading introduction)
Ms Eileen Tweedie (photography)
Ms Carole Blake (London Syndication)

Photographic Acknowledgments

Colour plates are in **bold type**. a – above, b – below, c – centre, l – left, r – right.

Collection Robin de Beaumont: **36**, 72, 77, 86; Biblioteca Civica, Bergamo: 20; Bibliothèque Nationale, Paris: 16a, 21, 85; Bodleian Library, Oxford: 16b (Ms Ash 1525 f. 111r), **17b** (Ms Kennicott 1 f. 447r), 52 (U.A. WP/25c/1 f. 205r); British Museum: 27; By courtesy of Jonathan Cape Ltd: 96b; Devon and Exeter Institution Library: **36a, 60a**, 76; Fitzwilliam Museum, Cambridge: 19; Collection Alison Harding: 58b, 62r, 63, 68, **69b**, **70**, 82r, 83; By permission of the Warden and Fellows of Keble College, Oxford: **18**; Marlborough Rare Books, London: 29, **35**, 49, 55, 57b, 61, 71, 73b, 75, 78, **79b**, 82; Private Collection: **79a**; Private Collection (Marlborough Rare Books, London): 8, 10, 26, 28, 30–34, 37–39, 40a, 40bl, 41–45, 53, 54l, 58a, 59, 60, 62l, 64–66, 73a; St Bride Printing Library, London: 23, 46b, 54r, 81, 90b, 94, 95b, 96ac; By courtesy of Sevenarts Ltd: **80a**; The Board of Trinity College, Dublin: **17a**; Victoria and Albert Museum, London: 11, 22–25, 46a, 47, 48, 50, 51, 56, 57a, 74, **80b**, 84, 89a, 91br; William Morris Gallery, London: 88; By courtesy of Mrs Betty Wyatt: 2.

Animated or patterned letters
are of special importance in early
manuscripts, where they not only
adorn the text but also indicate
divisions or points of interest
within it. In the 8th-century
French Gellone Sacramentary
several hundred coloured initials
are composed of fishes, birds and
beasts, often in conflict with
human figures. *Above*: St Michael
subdues the devil in serpent's
form, encircling the dotted S to
mark the beginning of the saint's
Office in the liturgy. *Below*: minor
initials from an English psalter of
the early 13th century depict
grotesque creatures; these are
confined within, rather than
actually forming, the letter shapes.

Opposite: at the beginning of the
Resurrection story from St Luke's
Gospel in the Book of Kells, the
dramatic curves of the central
initial and the angularity of the
letters below are emphasized by
the use of colour. The dynamic
zoomorphic design within the U is
balanced by the formal
arrangement of text and figures.
Below: the scribe of the Kennicott
Bible, a Hebrew codex of the 15th
century, uses a witty, cleverly
animated script; the complete
colophon reads: 'I Joseph son of
Hayim this book have pictured and
completed'.

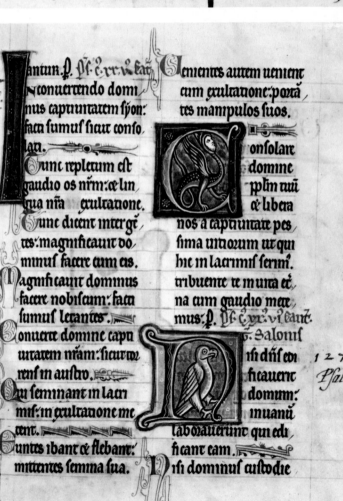

Some early pattern books for artists include designs for decorated initials: those above are from a complete, pen-drawn, 12th-century alphabet which on other pages shows both Roman and uncial letter forms. Their decorations are relatively restrained and simple to copy, incorporating Romanesque-style biting creatures.

In the initial (*above left*) of a German Cistercian missal, *c.*1300, grotesque elements are subordinate to formal patterns using two colours with striking effect. The style looks forward, particularly in the repetition of a 'lily-of-the-valley' motif, to designs used by 15th-century German printers. In contrast, the Beatus page (*below left*), from a breviary written in Italy in 1404 for the Abbot of Montecassino, demonstrates the richness and pictorial versatility typical of Italian illumination of this period. Elaborate acanthus scrolls enclose figures of Christ and David, surrounded by saints and angels, within the initial B, while minor letters are gracefully supported by winged cherubim.

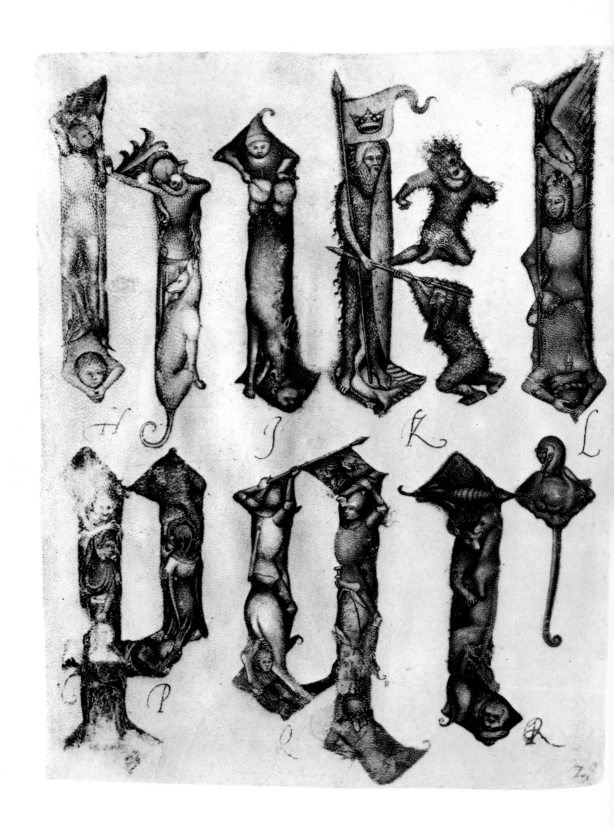

Naturalistic representation of birds, animals and human figures is evident in
alphabet designs of the later Middle Ages. The 'Bergamo' alphabet (*left*), thought to
be the work of Giovannino dei Grassi, *c*.1390, consists of delicately coloured letters
which, though purely Gothic in shape, owe much to the Romanesque zoomorphic
tradition, as well as to contemporary interest in natural forms. The letters h and q
shown here are among several imitated in an alphabet engraved on copper, *c*.1460,
by the master 'E.S.', one of a group of skilled artist-engravers working in Germany
and the Low Countries. The m (*above*) shows the detailed observation of facial
expression, costume, and bird or animal form characteristic of this artist, who uses
the angles of birds' wings to indicate the Gothic letter shape. Though grotesque or
fantastic in effect, such alphabets often included sacred subjects, such as the
Annunciation, in their compressed but vigorous representation of humans and angels,
and wild or domestic creatures.

ock en sult ghn nemants hups' naudte beghe'nen
Noch nemants goet tot e'emghe dieghe
Maint begherde remant het utte tfoude u derren
Maert datmen' deromme leide laeghen
Dus vint ghn dat hn mach God behaeghen
Die hem bouen al kennnt alsoot behoort
En sn naesten als hem seluen om puerer confoort

Duure' mes' vrae que ne mendurme
Ang poche gn sut eneeme
Este en my toute ambition
Tout orgueff et presumption

Samel kinder die Wel comen lesen ende scryuen
sut men in Ryckdom alder meest bedryuen

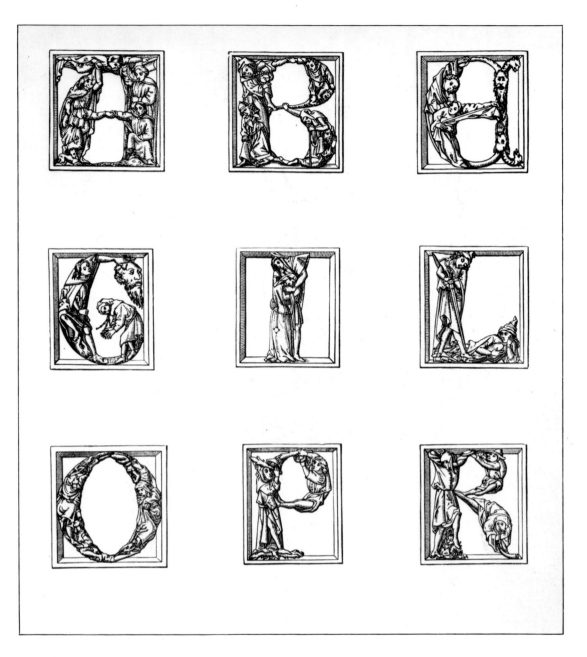

Fantasy and reality are combined in this meticulously drawn alphabet of Marcus van Ypres, whose work, produced *c*.1500, exemplifies the grotesque letter tradition of the Low Countries. A dentist and his apprehensive patients appear in the O (*left*); other letters depict huntsmen, merchants and ladies, with mythical beasts and figures which, like the lattice and scroll decorations, feature also in many contemporary initials.

Some of the original humour and vigour is lacking in the 19th-century refinement (*above*) of a famous alphabet known in several versions, including the woodcut 'Basle alphabet' of 1464, and another engraved by the contemporary 'Master of the Banderoles'. The Whittingham sisters and Mary Byfield probably used a 16th-century English copy for these initials reproduced in the catalogue of the Chiswick Press (see also p. 90).

A A B B B C C C D D D E F F
F F G G G H H H I K K K
X L L M M M N N N
O O O P P P Q Q Q R
R S S S T T V V V V
W V V W X X Y V Z 1

DESEUSE NOT A MAN THAT TURNED
HUM SELFE A WAYE FROM SUNNE
AND CASTE HUM NOT IN THE TETH W
ALL BUT REMEMBRE V WE AR FRAYLE
EUERICHONE R H

ROBERT THOHS MARCER

The art of the copyist, so important in the production of letters for illuminated manuscripts, contributed to the extensive circulation of alphabet designs in the 15th and 16th centuries. The letters h and I (*above*), which accompany complete Roman and Gothic alphabets respectively, are taken from one of several decorated alphabets in an English manuscript writing-book of *c*.1550. Produced by an unknown scribe (possibly the Robart Ihons whose name and initials appear on some pages, including the h shown here), the designs illustrated first appeared in the work of Noel Garnier, a contemporary artist whose alphabets were engraved in France and widely copied. His style reflects both Romanesque influence and Renaissance interest in the human figure: serpents and birds, mermaids and cherubs accompany knights, ladies and peasants, with decorations of naturalistic flowers and leaves, scrolls and interlacing. An ambiguous figure, reminiscent of the mythical 'Green Man' of late medieval literature, forms the stem of the h; while the naked men supporting the branches of the I have much in common with the 'human alphabets', featuring athletes and Venuses, that were produced by Peter Flotner and his imitators (see p. 46) in Germany, France and Italy in the later 16th century.

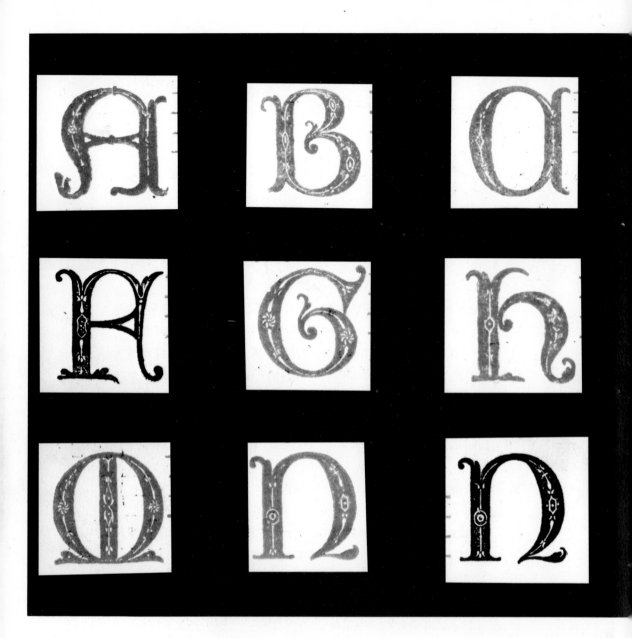

Hand-drawn and painted initials appeared in the earliest printed books, including the first extant book printed in Italy, the *De Oratore* of Cicero, illustrated here (*right*). Produced at Subiaco by Sweynheim and Pannartz in 1464–65, this was the first book in Roman type, the bold clarity of which is matched by the abstract design of the initial M. The fine pen-work decoration of this letter, though relatively restrained, is characteristic of the work of scribes whose artistry was soon to be superseded by the use of initials engraved on blocks and printed with the text. Those illustrated above, printed in red and black in a late 15th-century missal, retain something of the quality of hand-painted letters; the blurred outlines indicate that, though cut on wood, they may have been stamped or pressed by hand rather than in a printing-press.

et cum exurgeret simul arridens: neq3 enim inquit tam mihi
molestus fuit: quod ius nostrum ciuile peruellit: q̃ iocundus
quod se id nescire confessus est .

AGNA nobis pueris Quite frater si me-
moria tenes opinio fuit. L. crassum nõ plus
attigisse doctrine: q̃ q̃tum p̃ma illa puerili
institutione potuisset: M. autẽ antoniũ õio
omnis eruditionis experte; atq3 ignarum
fuisse: Erantq3 multi qui q̃q̃ non ita sese rem b̃re arbitrarent
: tamen quo facilius nos incensos studio discendi a doctrina
deterrerẽt libenter id quod dixi de illis oratoribus predi-
carent: ut si boies nõ eruditi summã essent prudentiam atq3
incredibilem eloquentiã consequuti: inanis õnis noster esset
labor & stultum in nobis erudiendis p̃ris nostri optimi ac
prudentissimi uiri studium uideretur . Quos tum ut pueri
refutare domesticis testibus patre &.C. aculeone p̃pinquo
nostro et.L. cicerone patruo solebamus: quod de crasso p̃ et
aculeo quo cũ erat nostra matertera: quẽ crassus dilexit ex
omnibus plurimum et patruus qui cum antonio in ciliciam
p̃fectus una decesserat: multa nobis de eius studio doctrina sepe narrauit: Cumq3 nos cũ consobrinis nr̃is aculeonis
filiis & ea disceremus que crasso placerẽt: et ab his docto-
ribg qbus ille uterẽt erudiremur : etiã illud sepe itelleximg
cum essemus eiusmodi: quod uel pueri sentire poteramus:
illum & grece sic loqui nullam ut nosse aliam linguã uiderẽt
et doctoribus nr̃is ea ponere in percontando eaq3 ipe omni

Flower and leaf designs frequently reflect contemporary interest in botanical detail as well as conscious development by Renaissance artists of the decorative potential of winding stems, leaf arrangements, and petal shapes. Carefully executed examples from Lyons (*above*) combine accurate observation with generously proportioned Gothic letters; others, also from the early 16th century, show more stylized floral motifs and the increasingly popular Roman letterforms. Less delicate, Germanic initials of this kind (*bottom*) influenced some late 19th-century woodcut letters incorporating elongated forms and stem-like interlace: a pansy motif like that in the A was often used by Charles Ricketts, while the M is one of a set of initials copied from the 'Missale Traiectenso' (1515) by Henry Shaw, and known to Gothic Revival designers.

This page (*right*), printed at Reggio Emilia (by Ugo Ruggeri?) *c.*1500, from an edition of 'Quintus Curtius', shows how, at this immensely active period in printing, worn or unsuitable initials might appear even in conjunction with finely produced Roman text. The inverted A used as a V is a much-copied Venetian leaf design.

is nostris(quis suspectus in præteritum)ueniam ex pœ-
nitentia impetret. Sine auctore uero propositi libelli nul-
lo crimine locum habere debent. Nam & pessimi exem-
pli nec nostri seculi est.

¶ De plathea Amastrianorum.   LXII.

Mastrianorum ciuitas domine & elegans & or
nata habet inter præcipua opera pulcherrimā
eandemq; longissimam platheam:cuius a late-
re per spacium omne porrigitur nomine quidem flumē:
re uero cloaca fœdissima:ac situ turpis:imundissimo aspe
ctu:ita pestilens odore teterrimo. Quibus ex causis: non
minus salubritatis q̄ decoris interest ea contegi. Quod
fiet:si permiseris curantibus nobis:ne desit quoq; pecu-
nia operi tam magno q̄ necessario.

Ationis est mi Secūde charissime cōtegi aquā
istam:quæ per ciuitatem amastrianorum fluit:
si intecta salubritati obest. pecunia(ne huic ope
ri desit)curaturum te secundum diligentiam tuam certū
habeo.

¶ Votorum nuncupatio iri.   LXIII.

Ota domine priorum annorum nuncupata ala
cres lætiq; persoluimus:nouaq; rursus curante
cōmilitonum & prouincialium pietate suscepi-
mus:precati deos:ut te Remq;publicam florentem & in
columen ea benignitate seruarent: quam super magnas
plurimasq; uirtutes præcipua sanctitate obsequi deorum
honore mernisti.

Preoccupation with the human form and its activities, whether exemplified in classical legend, history or contemporary life, rapidly became evident in printed letter decoration. *Above*: clothed and naked figures set against interiors and landscapes appear in mid-16th-century initials from the Egenolff printing house at Frankfurt, source of many popular German designs, often using sharp-seriffed Roman letters in conjunction with finely detailed engraving. In some justly famous initials produced in Siena (*top, left and right*), classical nymphs, satyrs and cupids, or

figures from Roman history are combined with typical Italianate ornamentation. The letters, some printed in red, others formed from 'fish' or 'leaf' patterns, incorporate Renaissance grace without the restrictiveness imposed by the theorists.

In the Hebrew initials (*above*), *c.*1500, contemporary domestic scenes form the background for woodcut letters. The realism shown here is in direct contrast to the animated manuscript letters of earlier grotesque traditions, as seen in the example from the Kennicott Bible.

A marked freedom of expression coupled with technical skill characterizes 16th-century Venetian printing. Widely influential from the early days of Ratdolt and Aldo Manuzio, designs originating in Venice rapidly moved away from Gothic forms, yet letters continued to utilize traditional decorative themes in highly accomplished engraving. The large initials (*right*), designed early in the century but printed in a graduale of 1583, show woodcut Biblical scenes enclosed within frames of heavy scrolls and grotesque faces. The scales and fish-tails, leaves and tendrils are, however, carried over into the initials (*above*) printed in 1569 by Francesco or Giacomo Sansovino. Here serpents, monsters and half-human figures are transmuted into delicate yet energetic letters extending into the surrounding decoration. The vigour and expressive realism evident in the earlier religious themes of the graduale 'miniatures' seem to have moved outward to the letters themselves, which despite their classical lines are far less static than those of the graduale.

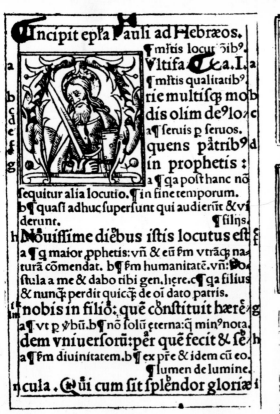

The commercial centre of Lyons played an important part in the interchange of ideas apparent in early printing. By 1500 more than 160 printers had worked in the city, many of them German. Renaissance artists and craftsmen travelled widely, exchanging blocks and type; the woodcut initials (*above*) from a Bible printed at Lyons in 1529 by Jacques Mareschal are typical of work showing several influences. Similar decorative pillars, scrolls and grotesques appear in contemporary German and Flemish letters, while the pictures of saints and apostles, simply drawn, appear in other French and German Bibles of the period, in a style already becoming superseded in Paris by more innovative design at the presses of Simon de Colines and the Estiennes.

Facsimiles of medieval letters appear in most 19th-century alphabet books; few are as faithful to the original as those drawn, engraved and hand-coloured by Henry Shaw (*right*) for his influential *Illuminated Ornaments from Manuscripts of the Middle Ages*, published by Pickering in 1833. The original alphabet appeared in a volume 'containing trees, flowers and animals painted on vellum [which] seems to have been a specimen-book of an illuminator or designer of pageants about the year 1500'. Sir Frederick Madden, who wrote the descriptions for Shaw's book, rightly noted the influence of Romanesque animated letters in the designs, but added the Victorian comment that 'the barbarous remains of this taste degenerated into mere grotesque'.

Much simpler in style is the 13th-century Gothic alphabet (*below right*) from the chromo-lithographed *Alphabet-Album* of Joseph-Balthazard Silvestre (Paris 1843). Together with the *Galerie* of Jean Midolle (1835) this work had a comparable influence on letter design in France to the work of Shaw and Owen Jones in England.

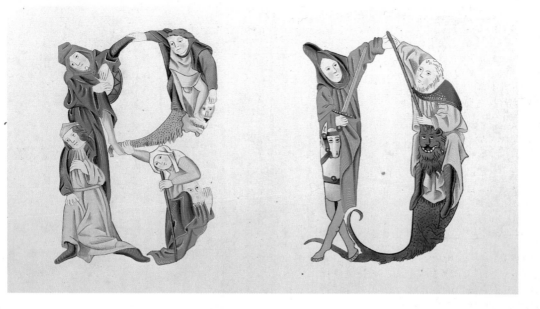

MAT
THE
VS

EX IUDAEA
SICUT IN ORDINE PRIMUS PONITUR
ITA EUANGELIUM IN IUDEA PRIMUS
SCRIPSIT CUIUS UOCATIO AD DM̄
EX PUBLICANIS ACTIBUS FUIT DUORŪ
IN GENERATIONE XPI PRINCIPIA PRAE
SUMENS UNIUS CUIUS PRIMA
CIRCUMCISIO IN CARNE ALTERIUS
CUIUS SECUNDUM COR ELECTIO FUIT
ET EX UTRISQUE IN PATRIBUS XP̄I

¶ Libzo tercero dela bistoria dela
iglesia.
Capi· Primero
de la gran tribulacion y cruel hã-
bze delos Judios.

Espues que Nero
poz treze años tu-
uo tiranizado el in
perio Romano: y
despues de sus suf
cessozes Galba y

Otho, que imperaron solo vn año
y seis meses: suscedio enel imperio
Vespasiano: q ala sazon cõquistaua
la tierra delos Judios: y poz el mes
mo exercito a quiẽ capitaneaua fue
coronado Empadoz. El ql luegose
partio pa Roma: y dexo encargada
la guerra a Tito su hijo. Ya era tiem
po que allende dela gloriosa victo
ria de nuestro saluadoz celebrada
C iij

Portuguese printed initials produced by Alvarez at Coimbra in 1569 (*above*) show
none of the Renaissance innovations of contemporary printing. By this time even
Spain, isolated like Portugal from the mainstream of European book production, was
adopting Roman types and classical styles of decoration. In the larger initials, the
grotesque birds, beasts and faces combined with scrolled letter shapes are similar to
those of incunabula produced by German printers, whose styles were brought to
Spain and Portugal at the end of the 15th century. But the elongated tendrils and
slender curves, evident particularly in the smaller, simpler initials, are distinctive,
while the 'bastarda' type used is more graceful than its heavier Germanic
counterparts.

Victorian illumination is seen at its most accomplished in the initial M (*left*) by
Owen Jones. When this page appeared in an issue of *The Illuminator's Magazine*
(1861–62) the artist's most important work, *The Grammar of Ornament*, had already
been published (1856), containing his researches into and reproductions of
manuscript letters, used as inspiration for his own designs.

Criblé or 'dotted' backgrounds appear frequently in pictures and initials engraved and printed in France around the end of the 15th century. Some particularly fine, well-known examples came from the Paris press of Gering and Rembolt (*right*); these, printed *c*.1495, show human figures, both secular and Biblical, with grotesques and different kinds of flower or foliage, in balanced designs which, though frequently imitated, are among the most effective in early printing. Ulrich Gering was one of three printers brought from the Rhineland to work the first press in France, at the Sorbonne, under the supervision of university academics who helped establish the reputation of Paris as a centre for fine printing. Religious books, in particular, were produced here, and later at Rouen, from where they were exported to England. The initials (*above*) from a missal printed either at Paris or Rouen, *c*.1510, contain detailed scenes and expressive human faces, with the criblé background and flowers of the Gering and Rembolt initials, but the actual letters are less striking, more conventional. The B (*above left*), shown in conjunction with clear, well-set type, is unusual in its portrayal of the Trinity, within an effective, uncluttered letter shape.

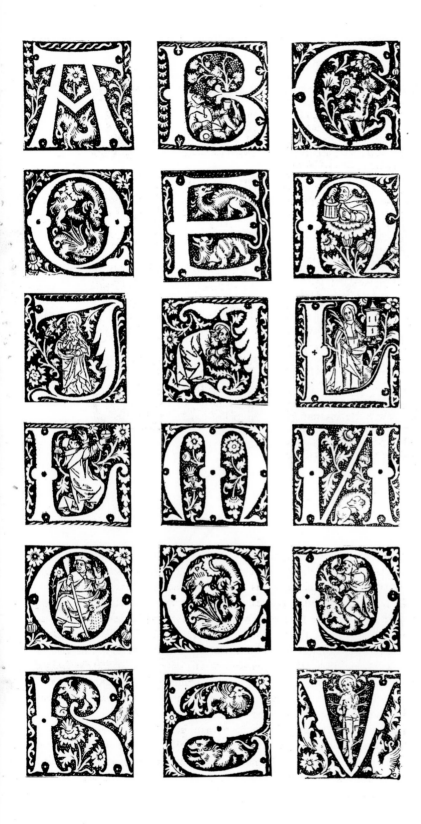

39

 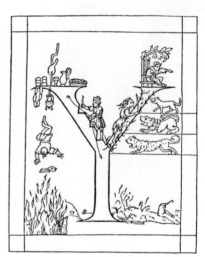

The letter designs of Geofroy Tory, highly influential in the establishment of Renaissance styles in French book decoration, owe much of their charm and distinction to his adoption of Italianate ornamentation. The influence of Italian humanism is evident in his widely circulated treatise on language and letterforms, *Champ Fleury*, in which the mathematical proportions of Roman letters are described. The initials *c.*1532 (*above*) show these letters on a familiar French criblé background, with delicate traceries of leaves and flowers in the Italian manner. The larger P is interesting for its pierced letter and sinewy entwined stems, like those used by Lucien Pissarro in the early 20th century. More robust (*above*), later designs attributed to Tory show classical cornucopia and centaurs, as well as

monkeys and hares, among the trailing foliage. Others printed in Paris by Robert
Estienne in the 1540s, though formal, lack the restraining lines at the edges of the
blocks, and are energetic, almost exuberant, in effect. Tory's letter Y (*left*) from his
decorated alphabet in *Champ Fleury*, demonstrates both his concern with the theory·
of letters and his interest in allegorical decoration.

Children, animals and 'putti' were popular in German initial designs of the first half of the 16th century. Both Holbein and Dürer produced such alphabets, probably using earlier Venetian letters as their models. The A (*below*) is one of a set of letters by Hans Weiditz; much copied, and often attributed to Dürer, these are beautifully engraved, unlike many of the debased versions that followed. Anton Woensam's alphabet (*above*) incorporates plants and trees in the background; Peter Quentel, who printed this in 1533, had a few years before secretly produced at Cologne some pages of the translation by William Tyndale of the New Testament, the first in English, and the cause of Quentel's sudden flight to Worms. Anton Woensam also produced woodcuts for a Catholic Bible printed at Mainz, in a period of intense activity and mobility among German printers and craftsmen.

In a much later, 17th-century alphabet (*right*), thought to be from the Low Countries, the distinctive spiky letters of the German initials are replaced by shadowed, less angular forms. Though cherubs and some grotesque faces remain as part of the background, the foliate decorations are more important here, resembling those of Kilian's alphabet (see p. 49).

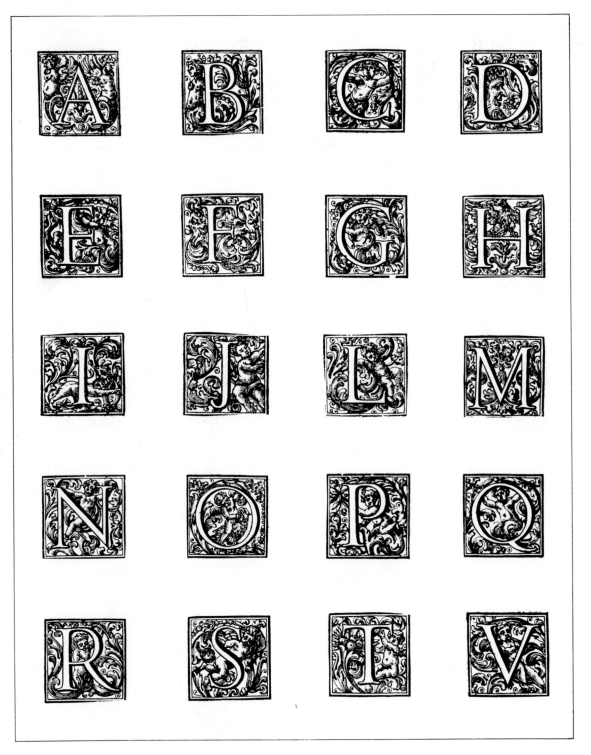

Dutch 'flower-pot' initials of the early 17th century (*right*) are among the more pleasing, less derivative designs found at a period when political and religious ferment contributed to a general decline in European printing. While masters of calligraphy developed their artistic talents in highly decorated writing-books, repetition of familiar designs, often with worn or badly copied blocks, made printed initials look dull and superfluous. In Germany and England, learning and politics dominated at the expense of visual arts; but in the Low Countries, craftsmen still produced finely engraved printed letters, which were less static in design than those influenced by French decorative styles, predominant since the time of Tory. Some graceful, more original arabesque patterns, however, began to appear elsewhere in conjunction with dignified, shadowed Roman letters, like those (*above*) from an English edition of Camden's *Brittania* (*c.*1630).

Incarnatio

423
1152
13

Anne Christi 1588

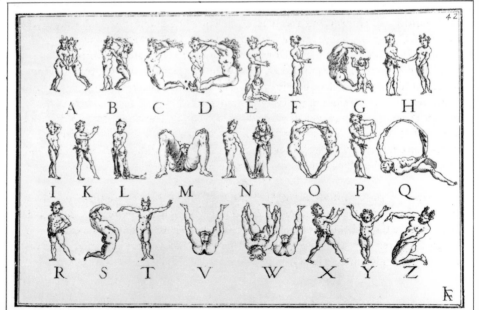

A B C D E F G H

I K L M N O P Q

R S T V W X Y Z

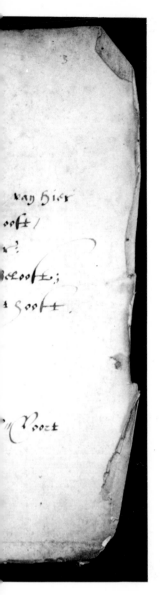

Arabesques and interlacing combine in the complex, graceful letter A designed
for an *ABC pour la jeunesse* (*above left*), produced in Holland in the late 16th
century. The author, Aert van Meldert, was apparently a French schoolmaster
working in Rotterdam; his purpose in publishing the book seems to have been the
display of his own skill alongside instructional verses and precepts intended for his
young pupils, rather than the provision of calligraphic models for copying, in the
manner of the great writing-masters of the time. Van Meldert's letters appear in a
variety of styles, some interlaced and with birds or animals among the flourishes,
others more formal, like the H above, incorporating urns with leaves or flowers and
criblé or 'dotted' infilling similar to the decorations of contemporary printed initials.

Anthropomorphic alphabets, of the kind engraved by G. Franco (*left*) in Italy at
the end of the 16th century, appeared first in Germany with the designs of Peter
Flotner (1534), which were much imitated. Later versions include an ingenious
design by Silvestre, which continues the Renaissance conception of perfect figures
used to create ideal letter shapes.

47

Natural history and contemporary pastimes appear in two outstanding
alphabets of late Renaissance Germany. That of the brothers Johan Theodore and
Johan Israel de Bry (1595) (*above*) depicts flora and fauna, exotic and familiar, with
angular, metallic-looking letters. The regular shape and accurate detail of the
engravings suggest that the alphabet was possibly intended for use in the massive
topographical work on the Indies compiled by T. de Bry the elder.

    Lucas Kilian's *ABC Buechlein* shows large, exuberant letters (*right*) with pictures
of children engaged in music-making, book-binding, sculpture, tailoring and even
learning their ABC. Regina Hertlerin, a cabinet-maker's daughter, engraved this
1632 edition at Augsburg; 19th-century versions lose some of the original vigour of
Kilian, considered the pre-eminent designer of ornament of this period in Germany.

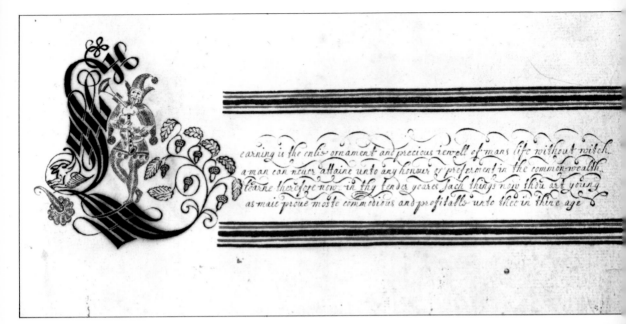

An English copy book, written out *c.*1690 by a writing-master's pupil, possibly John Stonestreet, shows initials and scripts copied from the first writing-book printed in England. This, *A Booke Containing Divers Sortes of Handes* (1571), included among its French and English examples the difficult 'lettres frizées' (*top left*) and flowing italic (*top right*) which accompany the latticed initial letters. Stonestreet's decorative figures are skilfully executed, especially the archer, a version of those that sometimes appear in illuminated letters.

English writing-masters of the 17th century were numerous, and often quarrelsome. Among them, Edward Cocker was one of the most skilful and prolific, writing and engraving books including *The Pen's Transcendencie*, 1654, from which a

typically witty, complex page appears above; its initial N is, true to tradition, accomplished in an unbroken line. Less sophisticated in style, and looking back to the grotesque letters of the artist-scribes like Marcus van Ypres (see p. 22), the initial C (*left*) comes from the writing-book of an unknown English master, *c*.1600.

Portraits within initials, often used in illuminated manuscripts for dedication to a patron or monarch, were chiefly seen in legal documents by the 17th century, although pictures of writing-masters also appeared occasionally among their decorative flourishes. The portrait of Charles I (*above*), enclosed within a white-line engraving of his initial, comes from the manuscript of the Laudian Statutes approved for the use of Oxford University in 1636. The accomplished embellishments of the letter would have been appreciated by the King, once a pupil of the master Martin Billingsley, who dedicated to him his book *The Pen's Excellencie* of 1618.

Conventional calligraphic designs, based on those of the great writing-masters, appeared in some printed books as late as the 18th century; the initials shown here (*above right*) were printed by Cozens and Martier in Holland *c.*1710. Others (*below right*), far more original in conception, came from the press of J.J. Kamenik in Prague at about the same date. Some of these have detailed landscape backgrounds with figures and flowers; others show humour and ingenuity in fitting human features within the curves of the letters, some of which are unusually dramatic in shape.

Florentine grace and artistry characterize the letters
C and D (*far right*) of an alphabet book designed by
Mauro Poggi. Pen-drawn by Andrea Bimbi and
engraved *c.*1730 by Lorenzo Lorenzi, this is regarded
as one of the most charming and versatile of 18th-
century alphabets, produced at a time when naturalistic
elements were once again emerging to add a new, much
needed liveliness to the decoration of letters. Birds,
flowers, animals and human figures are combined, often
wittily, with scrolled letters that retain classical delicacy
and strength.

The 'bloemen initials' (*right*) used by the revitalized
Oxford University Press in the late 17th century show
a calligraphic freedom and exuberance. Nicknamed
'Dutch bloomers', these have little in common with the
formal, 'flower-pot' initials popular in Holland. In
some respects their style is reminiscent of scrolled,
grotesque 16th-century initials, for example in the
upright stem of the R; and the use of a small motif to
break the line of the letter is also carried over from
early printing. But in spirit the 'bloomers', which exist
in both large and small versions, look forward to the
next century, as does the W (*above*) printed at Leipzig
*c.*1700. This letter shows a more naturalistic approach,
with its shape formed from a vine stem with leaves and
grapes; the flowing lines of the letter are unbroken
apart from a hardly discernible knot at the top and
bottom curves.

Mauro Poggi inv. e del.
Andrea Bimbi in penna

L. Lorenzi inc.

Mauro Poggi inv. e del.
Andrea Bimbi in penna

L. Lorenzi inc.

Fortuna assistimi.

Volgo il Pensiero a te volubil Dea
Che stringi in pugno le Province, e i Regni,
Proteggi me nella scabrosa idea
E spargi il tuo favor sù miei Disegni.

Sarò pieno di giubbilo
Diva da te protetto.
Mentre vedrò l'Invidia
Fremere al tuo cospetto.

DOVÈ LA SORTE
OGN' ALMA È FORTE.

Gaet. Giarré inc. dis. e inc. 1797

Detailed naturalism and calligraphic skill combine in the Alphabet Book (1797) of another Florentine artist-engraver, Gaetano Giarré. Each letter is part of a formally balanced page incorporating verses in different writing styles with drawings of birds and insects, reptiles, animals and flowers. Natural history often featured in 18th-century illustrated books intended for leisured perusal; both French and Italian book decoration show the precision and delicacy apparent in Giarré's letters, composed of scrolls and cornucopia, from which burgeon flowers, grasses and corn similar to those of Marillier (*opposite*).

The personality of the artist, given
little scope in most printed initial
designs at this time, is an important
factor in the highly individual alphabet
of the German T.A. Pingeling (*above*).
Engraved in 1780, his deceptively simple
letters create detailed scenes; in the L he
uses waves, a tree and a flight of seagulls
to form the letter shape, while the O and
A are almost surreal in effect. Pingeling's
contemporary, C.P. Marillier, who made
an important contribution to French
book illustration, applied accomplished
technique to his set of large monograms
(*left*). The minutely drawn flowers and
berries show why Marillier was called 'le
dessinateur de l'infiniment petit'.

The interrelation of calligraphy and printing is particularly close in the engraved title-pages and head- and tail-pieces of many books produced in the late 17th and early 18th centuries. While textual initials still reflected some of the now arid Renaissance theories of decoration, letters such as the R and D (*above*) in a head-piece by J.D. Preissler, engraved in Germany *c.*1700, fully realize their potential as pure ornament. Realistic creatures – birds, snakes, even a porcupine – harmonize with the abstract patterns of the letter shapes, which flow into the surrounding tendrils and scrolls. Also from Germany, the title-page (*opposite*) of a Life of Charles XII of Sweden, engraved by Jonas Haas in 1751, though technically impressive, seems over-elaborate when compared with examples of 18th-century Spanish calligraphic styles (*right*), reproduced in the *Schriften-Atlas* of Petzendorfer, 1894.

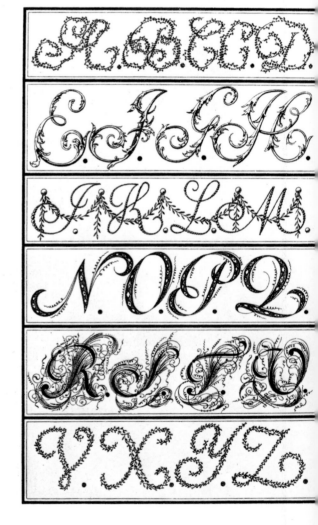

Leben

CARL

des Zwölften

Königs in Schweden

mit

Kupfern.

Gustav v. Sanden

Dritter Theil.

1751.

von Leipzig 1764

gestochen von Jonas Haas

Letters as trees must have seemed a novel conceit to the artist of the alphabet
shown above, only a few letters of which have survived. Probably engraved in Italy
in the mid-18th century, the designs have a repeated landscape background, against
which small figures assist in the felling operations by which each letter is formed.
The base of the E, the tree's shadow, may have been painted in, for the same
picture was used for the F.

Letters as architectural plans, an even greater feat of imagination, were produced
in the 1770s by J.D. Steingruber, architect and master-builder at Ansbach in
Bavaria. Dedicated to the Margrave Alexander and his consort, whose initials are
used as ground plans for a palace each, the *Architectural Alphabet* was conceived as a
serious exercise: a version of the M (*right*) ingeniously overcomes the problems of
difficult angles in the letterform.

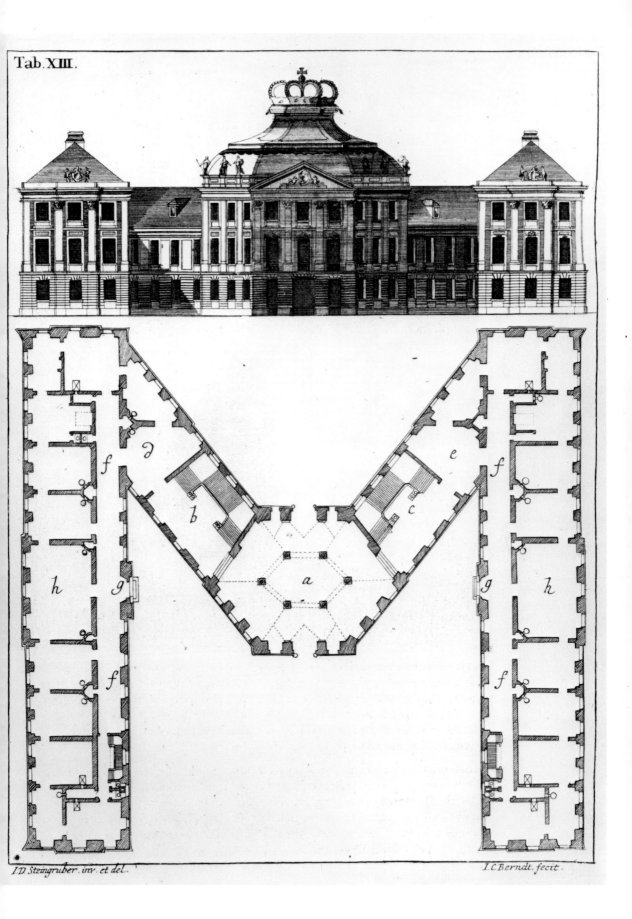

Tab. XIII.

I.D. Steingruber. inv. et del.

I.C. Berndt. fecit.

Dutch engravers working in England in the latter half of the 17th century contributed some finely executed initials, at a time when English printing was at a low ebb. The T (*above left*), engraved by Wenzel Hollar for the 1670 edition of John Ogilby's *Africa*, incorporates a globe and other equipment appropriate for the writings of a famous cosmographer; many initials appearing in books at this period bore no relation to the text, even when well done in other respects. An earlier work by Ogilby, his translation of Virgil, published in London in 1654, was decorated with initials designed by Franz Cleyn and also engraved by Hollar.

A set of classical and mythological scenes feature in letters designed by another Dutchman, Michael Burghers, for the Oxford University Press, for whom he worked throughout his career as engraver. Some of these initials appeared, inappropriately, in Clarendon's *History of the Rebellion*, 1707; others, including the L (*right*) were used in the *Grammaticus* of George Hickes, printed at the Sheldonian, also in 1707. The reclining figure is possibly Leander, having swum the Hellespont and being presented with a laurel wreath. Burghers also engraved the initial Q (*above*), after Raphael's 'Madonna della Sedia'; this too was used in Hickes's book, along with the numerous engravings of early letters, including Anglo-Saxon initials, which appeared in this important palaeographic work.

enim Reges ab ODINI,

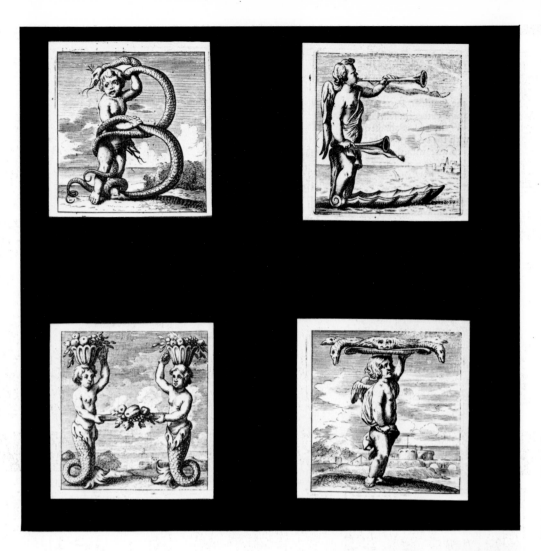

Myth, allegory and classical landscapes provide
themes for initials in some late 17th- and early 18th-
century books, in which illustrations played an
increasingly important part. Letters formed from
robust cherubs or mermaids (*above*), used in Richard
Blome's *Britannia* of 1673, show similarities to a
human alphabet with snakes, platters, fruit and fish
as part of the designs, printed in Bologna at about
the same time. Italian influence appears also in the
background to the G (*right*), an engraving by an
unidentified artist, in which Knowledge, supported
by a female figure, perhaps Giudicia, is keeping
Time at bay. More realistic landscapes, with
graceful, shadowed letters, are seen in the initials
(*far right*) of Luigi Vanvitelli, an Italian architect
and designer of the mid-18th century. Son of a
Dutch architect, Gaspard van Wittell, who settled in
Italy, he designed a palace for Pope Clement XII as
well as barracks, piazzas, and aqueducts.

L. Vanvitelli — Nolli s.

Vanvitelli — Nolli s.

L. Vanvitelli — Nolli s.

L. Vanvitelli — Nolli s.

L. Vanvitelli — Nolli s.

Travel and architecture, subjects of much interest to the well-educated reader of the early 18th century, feature in the pictorial initials produced at the press of Pieter van der Aa in Leyden *c*.1713. Publisher of the important *Opera Omnia* of Erasmus, van der Aa specialized in the production of maps, and also published in 1729 a sixty-volume work, *La Galerie Agréable du Monde*, which contained over a thousand copperplate engravings of travel, history and costume, drawings for which may have been used for some of his decorative initials. He and his brother Hildebrand also practised engraving, in a heavy style of which the M shown above may be an example. But the enlarged L (*right*) is the more skilful work of Jan van Vianen of

Amsterdam; he engraved many illustrations and contemporary portraits for books,
and the design for the L (*top left*) may be from his portrait of Frederick William of
Prussia. Another L (*top right*), similarly detailed in execution, is possibly by Vianen;
the T with cherubs, maps and a globe, is more probably the work of Pieter van
der Aa.

Colour printing on the handpress was the subject of *Practical Hints on Decorative Printing*, produced in 1822 by William Savage, who included in his book an ornamental letter B (*right, above*). The design, incorporating traditional scrolls and a dolphin, was engraved on wood and printed with seven blocks. Planned to show how colours and gold could be used in initials and illustrations, Savage's project proved uneconomic, if technically brilliant. The Byzantine letter (*right, below*), reproduced at the end of the century in Petzendorfer's *Schriften-Atlas*, shows how lithographic processes were used to achieve a similar end.

A revival in English printing came about in the mid-18th century, largely through the work of the typefounder William Caslon, who stopped the importing of Dutch types, establishing his own 'Old Face' Roman as the standard English type. This is seen here (*right*) in conjunction with an initial decorated in the Dutch style, reproduced, as was the classical A (*above*), in a retrospective catalogue printed by the Caslon firm in 1924.

HE
exc
Fac
con
has
prir
the
present ın a new way this
Face Types, which were
Caslon the First, Englanc

Petzendorfer, Schriften-Atlas.

Red. Hochhaase, Stuttgart.

Verl. v. Jul. Hoffmann, Stuttgart.

Nach dem Breviarium Cassinense in der Bibliothèque Mazarine zu Paris.

Petzendorfer, Schriften-Atlas

Emil Hochdanz, Stuttgart.

Verl. v. Jul. Hoffmann, Stuttgart.

Nach Originalzeichnungen von E. Terschak.

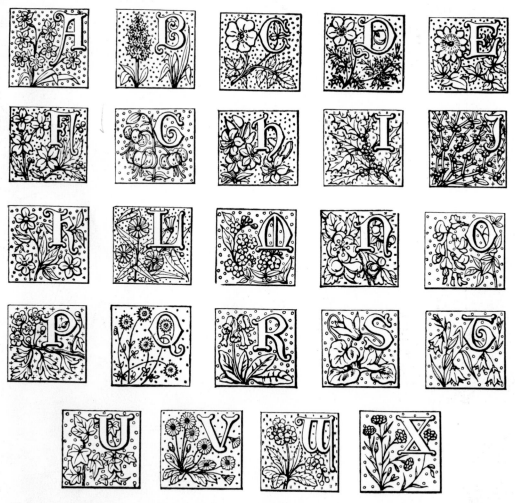

Conscious archaism in letter designs is evident in alphabet books and printers' catalogues of the later 19th century. The floral initials (*above*), from the 1890 catalogue of the Leadenhall Press, incorporate the criblé or 'dotted' background and some flower motifs – pansy, cyclamen and lily – of 16th-century designs; but the letters are Gothic Revival rather than the authentic reproduction found in the flower initials copied by the Whittinghams for the Chiswick Press (see pp. 23 and 90). Factotums printed from old blocks, children's alphabets, and many 'antique style' letters appear in Leadenhall Press books, which tried to recover the vigour and boldness of early woodcut and printing.

'German Renaissance' flowers and children with Gothic-style letters appear (*left*) in an alphabet reproduced in the *Schriften-Atlas* of Ludwig Petzendorfer, printed in Stuttgart in 1894. The many coloured lithographed plates, the accurate engraving of such historic alphabets as those by Kilian and J.T. de Bry, and the presentation of modern display letters, including 'sans serif' and 'shadowed' styles, make this an important collection. The chief preoccupations of those involved in 19th-century printing and book-production are reflected here: antiquarian and aesthetic interest in letters of the past, combined with the use of new techniques in the mass production of printed material.

The Romantic imagination seems to have found expression even in alphabet
books and initial designs. *The Landscape Alphabet* (*above*) of 1825, lithographed from
stone in England where this process had recently arrived from Germany, uses letter
shapes to show people and animals in relation to sea, sky, trees and ruins; some
letters, like the P and E shown here, look back to late 18th-century pastoral or
Gothic themes, but the predominant mood is that of Wordsworth's poems. Possibly
the artist, named Jones, knew Pingeling's more compressed designs, which the S and
L of this alphabet resemble.

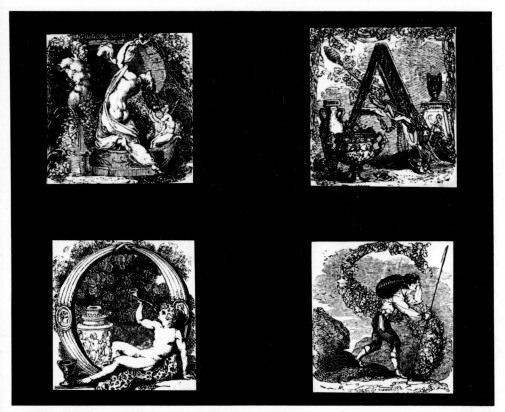

An emphasis on line characterizes this alphabet book (*left*) designed by Achille Deveria and lithographed *c.*1858 by Lemercier for the publisher Delarue in Paris. The gracious proportions of the letter, the half-human figures and foliate decorations, the Grecian urn of Keats's poem, all contribute to a spirit of nostalgic classicism. More energetic in expression, the initials by an unknown French designer (*above*) of about the same time place classical figures – lacking any obvious connection with the adjacent letters – in detailed settings. The letters, composed of flowers, pillars, archways and trees, are typical mid-century extravaganzas.

73

Contemporary allusions appear most often in children's alphabets: possibly the French and Portuguese examples shown here were meant for children, though as gifts rather than for schoolroom use. Engraved by Tellier for Andrew, Best & Leloir of Paris in 1833, the earlier (*right*) presents impressive shadowed letters against a design of baroque-style ornament. Here Napoleon is accompanied by Neptune, nymphs and a negro, while on a facing page Minerva is poised on a monument, with masks and a mandarin below.

In the late 19th-century *Alphabet Aboim* of Consuelo Godhino, engravings of familiar scenes or figures (*opposite*) accompany almost rococo letters, chromolithographed in delicate tints, with silver or gold heightening the Spanish-style patterned ground. Consuelo's sister Laura also designed an alphabet book containing, like this one, the artist's portrait.

Antiquarian interest in letter designs resulted in a number of 19th-century scholarly works, among the earliest of which was Thomas Astle's *The Origin and Progress of Writing* (1803). Keeper of the Records in the Tower of London, Astle was concerned with the movement and changes of early letterforms; but his many engravings, though less faithful to the originals than copies of initials and alphabets by Shaw or Silvestre, show essential details. His drawings (*above*) from the 7th-century 'Textus Sancti Cuthberti' reproduce the dotted decorations and interlacing, spirals and biting creatures of Anglo-Saxon letters; but the technical accomplishment of these was inevitably inferior to later chromolithographic reproductions.

Illuminated letters in Victorian books, inspired by the work of artists like Owen Jones and Noel Humphreys, led to a vogue for hand-colouring by amateurs. Popular manuals encouraged this, providing line drawings as models or for practice; but for the serious practitioners, and for scholars, a superior periodical, *The Illuminator's Magazine*, appeared in 1861–62. It included drawings by Humphreys of Celtic initials (*right*), finely detailed and authentic, showing their construction as well as their decoration. Chromolithographed by Day & Son, one among several English firms to master the new process, the magazine made a useful contribution to the upholding of standards at a period of much imitation and rapid popularization in design of all kinds.

Plate XIII

1

2

3

4

London, Day & Son, lith.rs to the Queen, 1862

Innovative letters in unusual materials appear in the *Album de Lettres* of E.A. Ducompex, issued in Paris in 1880. Here the Egyptian, shadowed and rustic types of so many 19th-century catalogues are transformed into many-coloured 'lettres de fantaisie', made from bamboo, metal balls, tubes or pipes, casting heavy shadows or seen from unexpected angles; the letter is now an independent three-dimensional object, which, though 'fantastic' in some respects, has its purpose in display, on buildings, shop fronts and commercial advertising. Such designs as the 'lettres bois' (*above*) made, so Ducompex insists, from *broken* pieces of wood nailed together to achieve the correct angles for the letter shapes, are more practical and forward-looking than was evident when they were first conceived. The 'lettres tubulaires' (*top*) are particularly modern in style, and carefully arranged to achieve the rounded curves of the components as well as of the letterforms; while the heavily gilded 'lettres monstres perspectives' (*below right*) are arranged to be seen from below, to give their full architectural effect.

'Jewelled' and embossed letters, popular in the mid-19th century, are used for a charming 'scrap' alphabet (*top right*). Printed by chromolithography, probably by one of the numerous German or English firms specializing in the production of coloured scraps and cards in the 1860s, the letters show the 'Tuscan' fish-tail serifs and 'jewel' motifs of some contemporary types. The pastoral designs of shepherdesses and flowers – roses, violets and forget-me-nots – suggest that the letters (each *c*.2cm in height) were intended for use on the hand-made Valentine cards of the period.

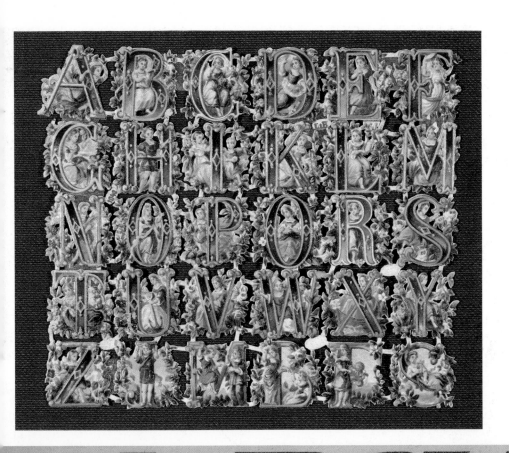

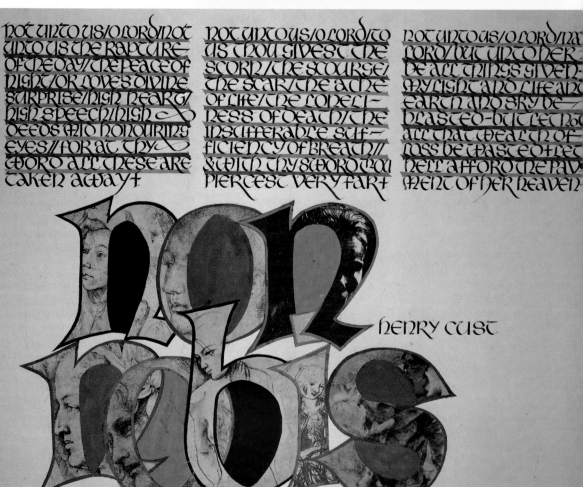

NOT UNTO US/O LORD/NOT UNTO US THE RAPTURE OF THE DAY/THE PEACE OF NIGHT/OR LOVES DIVINE SURPRISE/HIGH HEART/HIGH SPEECH/HIGH DEEDS MID HONOURING EYES//FOR AT THY WORD ALL THESE ARE TAKEN AWAY†

NOT UNTO US/O LORD/TO US THOU GIVEST THE SCORN/THE SCOURSE/THE SCAR/THE ACHE OF LIFE/THE LONELI-NESS OF DEATH/THE INSUFFERABLE SUF-FICIENCY OF BREATH//& WITH THY SWORD DOU PIERCEST VERY FAR†

NOT UNTO US/O LORD/NAY LORD/BUT UNTO HER/BE ALL THINGS GIVEN-MY LIGHT AND LIFE AND EARTH AND SKY BE-BLASTED-BUT LET NOT ALL THAT WEALTH OF LOSS BE WASTED/LET HELL AFFORD THE PAV-MENT OF HER HEAVEN

HENRY CUST

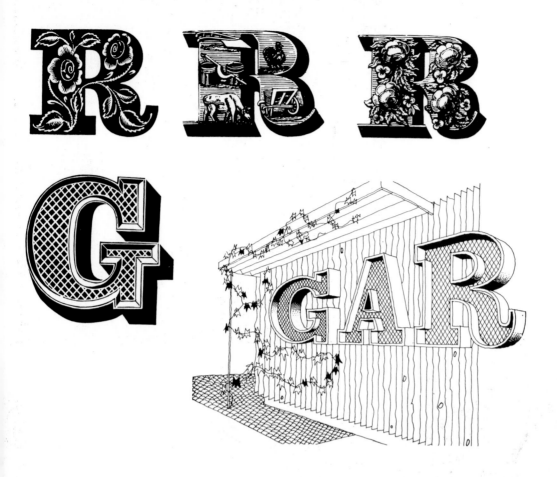

Changing styles in Victorian typefaces appear (*top*) in specimens from the foundries of Blake & Stephenson and Wood & Sharwood. Flat, broad surfaces of 'Egyptian' or 'fat face' letters, some casting heavy shadows, are decorated at first with simple flowers (1826), later with detailed farmyard motifs (1838), followed by fruit or flower designs executed in spirited fashion (1841). Ideal for display purposes, a checked version was adapted for official lettering at the Festival of Britain in 1951 (*above*).

A modern animated alphabet, art deco in mood but personal in style and conception, was created by the designer Erté, whose letter W appears (*above left*). Begun in 1927 and completed in 1967 for his London exhibition, the alphabet, in brilliant colours with black ground throughout, consists of large (40cm × 26.6cm) letters, including an L with a lady and leopard, one of Erté's most popular designs.

Calligraphic traditions used in new ways are shown in the design (*left*) for Henry Cust's 'Non Nobis . . .', produced in 1969 by Hella Basu. The outlining of the Gothic letters, with colours used as a foil to the fine drawing within and also to underline the lettering above makes this a particularly harmonious example of letter decoration.

Handbooks, manuals and primers containing alphabets abounded in the later 19th century. The 'Monumental' alphabet (*above*) appears in a little-known collection of 1858 by W.S. Ford, evidently intended for carvers or writers of inscriptions, though his examples are less authentic than he suggests. A 'Primer for the use of draughtsmen, surveyors, decorative painters, lithographers, engravers, carvers &c &c', engraved by F. Delamotte in 1872, includes the 'Rustic' alphabet (*far right*), an even spikier example than most of its kind, which was immensely popular. A more sober variant (*right*) features in the 1868 *Plain Words on the Art of Illuminating* by a Mrs Cooper, 'for ladies' who are informed that 'the art is not really difficult except for those who are colour blind.' *The Embroiderer's Alphabet* (Paris, 1905) shows letters adapted for use with drawn threads (*below right*), chiefly 'mock Gothic' in style; many copies of this book circulated in France, Germany, Italy and England.

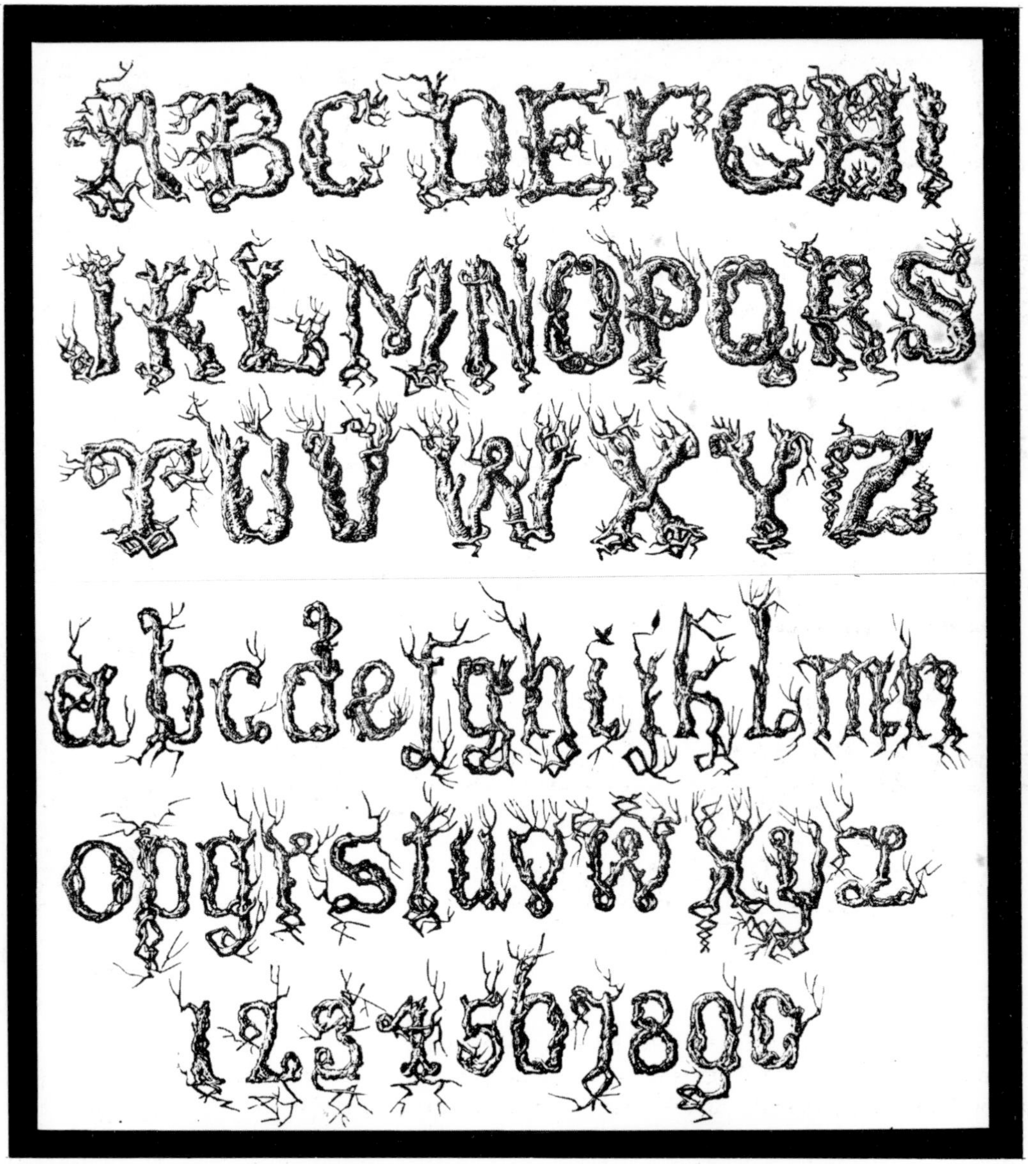

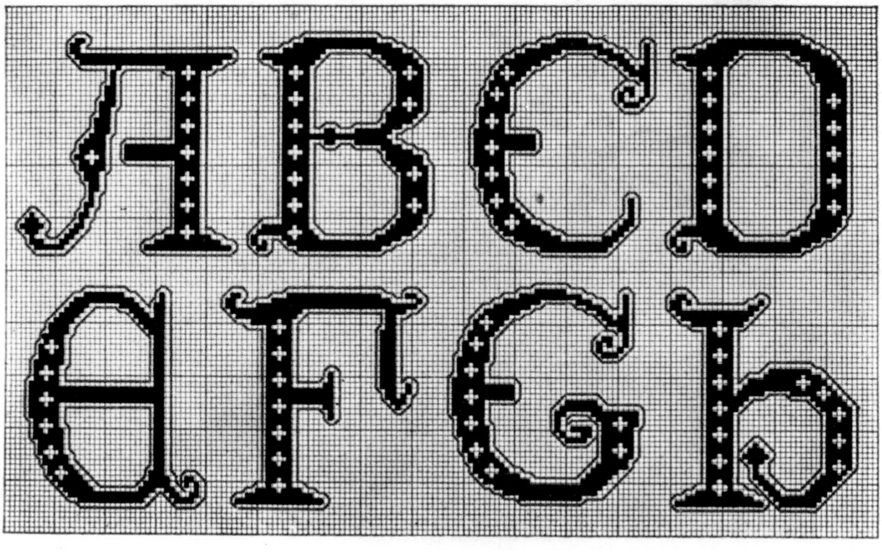

ABCDEFGHI
JKLMNOPQRS
TUVWXYZ

abcdefghijklmn
opqrstuvwxyz
1234567890

ABCD
EFGH

G g

H h

I i

J j

K k

L l

Alphabets for children acquired in the 19th century a sophistication lacking in earlier examples, intended for moral or instructional use rather than for pleasure. The *Alphabet Magique*, printed in Paris in 1861, combines education with amusement in its carefully engraved letters, traditional in style but placing the letter-associated objects or characters within the shape of each letter, in a fashion seen also in some 'scrap' alphabets of the period. Ingeniously, each letter incorporates a 'pull-out' device, used frequently in contemporary Christmas cards, so that the T, V, X and Z (*right*) slide out to reveal S, U, Y and X. The subjects within the letters are comparatively old-fashioned – classical figures, animals and familiar objects – and are captioned with appropriate verses, moral in tone.

The mood of Walter Crane's *Railroad Alphabet* of 1868, printed in bright reds, blues and greens, is more up-to-date, with its pictures of contemporary locomotives pulling into or departing from realistic termini. The letters are the bold Clarendons of Victorian railway typography, executed with equal care to that of the letters of the artist's later *Noah's Ark ABC* of 1872. The well-known *English Spelling Book*, drawn by Kate Greenaway and printed by William Mavor in 1885, shows less concern for the accuracy of letterforms but is entirely personal in conception, style and execution, a reason perhaps for its continued popularity.

Tour

T t — Tam-bour

sa se se se si so su
ta te té tè ti to tu

Soyez bon pour les malheureux
Tenez-vous toujours comme il faut

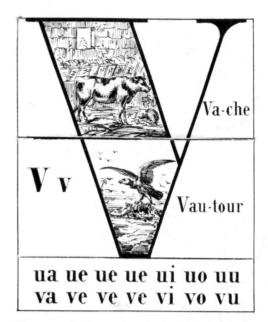

Va-che

V v — Vau-tour

ua ue ue ue ui uo uu
va ve ve ve vi vo vu

Unissez la douceur à l'amour de l'étude
Voltige, beau papillon, je saurai bien t'attraper

Xé-no-phon

X x — Xer-cès

wa we wé wè wi wo wu
xa xe xé xè xi xo xu

Williams est un petit garçon bien
élevé
Xercès, roi de Perse, fut assassiné
par Artaban

Z z — Zè-bre

Zi-be-li-ne

ya ye yé yè yi yo yu
za ze zé zè zi zo zu

York, ville d'Angleterre, nous fournit
d'excellents jambons
Zémire est le nom de ma petite chienne
et Azor celui de mon petit chien

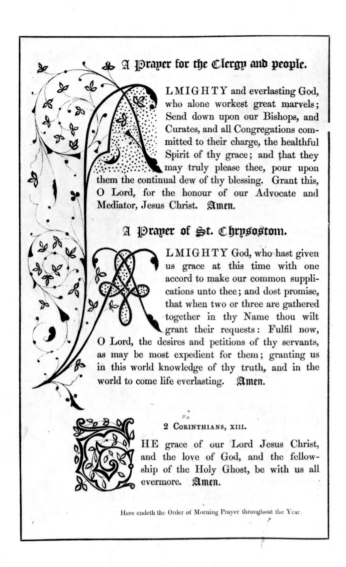

The **personal creative styles** of some Victorian artists found expression in decorative initials of high quality. Those of Owen Jones for *The Book of Common Prayer* (1845) show his capacity for integrating text and decoration (*above left*). Noel Humphreys's initial R (*above right*) for *The Months* (1864–65) reveals his preoccupation with natural history and his awareness of the potential of letters as patterned designs; the incorporation of initial within illustration, often disastrous in contemporary books, is successfully achieved here.

Gothic Revival style is combined with more innovative letters in William Morris's familiar wood-engraved design for his Kelmscott edition of Chaucer. Reproduced in a special number of *The Studio* (1914) devoted to book production of the period, this exemplifies the ideals of craftmanship upheld by the Morris School in reaction to the falling standards in design evident in many Victorian books. James Williams's initials (*below*) for the Vincent Press, also reproduced in *The Studio* of 1914, show, like Morris's minor letters, tendencies towards the spikier shapes of art nouveau styles, but are dominated by elements drawn from early printing – pierced letters, criblé backgrounds, trailing tendrils, leaves and flowers.

HERE BEGYNNETH THE PROLOGE OF SYR JOHAN FROISSART OF THE CHRONICLES OF FRAUNCE, INGLANDE, AND OTHER PLACES ADJOYNYNGE

The first Chaptre.

THAT the honorable and noble aventures of featis of armes, done & achyued by the warres of Fraunce and Inglande, shulde notably be inregistered, and put in perpetuall memory, whereby the prewe & hardy may haue ensample to incourage them in theyr well doyng, I, syr Johan froissart, wyll treat and recorde an hystory of great louage and preyse: but, or I begyn, I require the sauyour of all the worlde, who of nothyng created al thynges, that he wyll gyue me suche grace and vnderstandyng, that I may continue and perseuer in such wyse, that who so this proces redeth or hereth, may take pastaunce, pleasure, and ensaumple. It is said of trouth, that al buyldynges are masoned & wroughte of dyuerse stones, and all great ryuers are gurged and assemblede of divers surges and sprynges of water: in lyke wyse all sciences are extraught & compiled of diuerse clerkes, of that one wryteth, another parauenture is ignorant; but by the famous wrytyng of auncient auctours, all thyng is ben knowen in one place or other.

THAN to attaygne to the mater that I haue entreprised, I wyll begyn, fyrst, by the grace of God and the blessed Virgyn our Lady Saynt Mary, from whom all comfort and consolation procedeth, and wyll take my foundation out of the true cronicles somtyme compyled by the right reuerend, discrete and sage maister Johan la Bele, somtyme chanon in Saint Lambartis of Liege, who with good herte & due diligence dyd his true deuoure in wrytyng this noble cronicle, and dyd contynue it all his lyfes days, in folowyng the trouth as nere as he myght, to his great charge and coste in sekyng to procure and to haue the perfight knowledge thereof. He was also in his lyfes days welbeloued, and of the secret counsayle with the lorde sir Johan of Haynaulte, who is often remembred, as reason requyreth, here after in this boke: for of many fayre & noble auentures he was chiefe causer, & to the kyng right nigh, & by whose meanes the said syr Johan la Bele myght well knowe and here of many dyuers noble dedes. The whiche here after shal be declared.

TROUTH it is, that I who have entreprised this boke to ordeyne for pleasure and pastaunce, to the whiche alwayes I have been inclyned, & for that intent I haue folowed and frequented the company of dyuerse noble & great lordes, as well in Fraunce, Inglande, and Scotlande, as in diuerse other countries, and have had knowledge by them, and alwayes to my power iustly haue inquired for the trouth of the dedis of warre and auentures that haue fallen, and specially syth the great batell of Poytyers, where as the noble kynge Johan of France was takyn prisoner, as before that tyme I was but of a yonge age or vnderstandyng. Howe be it I toke it on me assoone as I come from scole, to wryte and recite the sayd boke, & bare the same compyled into Ingland, and presented the volume thereof to my Lady Phelyppe of Heynaulte, noble quene of Inglande, who right amyably receyved it to my great profite & avauncement.

AND it may be so, that the same boke is nat as yet examyned nor corrected so iustely as suche a case requyreth: for featis of armes derely bought & achyued, the honor therof ought to be gyuen & truly deuided to them that by prowes & hard trauayle haue deserued it. Therfore to acquyte me in that bihalfe, & in folowyng the trouth as near as I can, I, Johan froissart haue entreprysed this hystory on the forsaid ordynaunce & true fundacion, at the instaunce and request of a dere lorde of myn, Robert of Namure, knight, lorde of Bewfort, to whom entierly I owe loue and obeysaunce, & God graunt me to do that thyng that may be to his pleasure. Amen.

Here spekethe the auctour of suche as were most valiant knyghtis to be made mencion of in this boke. Capitulo II.

ALL noble hertis, to encorage & to shewe them ensample and mater of honour, I, Syr Johann froissart begynne to speke after the true report and relation of my master Johan la Bele, somtyme Chanon of Saynte Lambertis of

Decorated initial, border and text are conceived as parts of a unified page design in these examples by Morris, Beardsley and Ricketts. All three exploit the dramatic potential of black-and-white engraving, at the end of a century dominated by colour printing and by the illuminated rather than the wood- or metal-engraved letter. Apart from the distinguished productions of the Chiswick Press, Victorian books reflected a preoccupation with illustration rather than typography, an imbalance which William Morris sought to redress in his own book design at the Kelmscott Press. A trial page for an edition of Froissart's *Chronicles* (*left*) shows type and decoration in harmony, with the major initial T incorporated into the border in the style of illuminated manuscripts. However, the precision and intricacy of the engraved flowers and tendrils owe much to the techniques of the French and Italian Renaissance designers of initials, much admired by Morris.

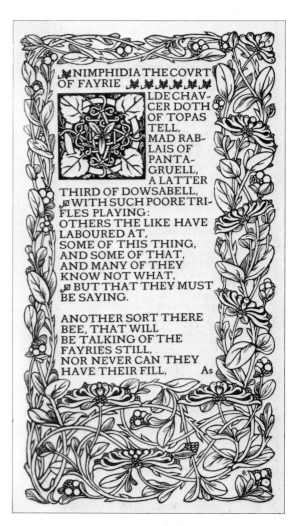

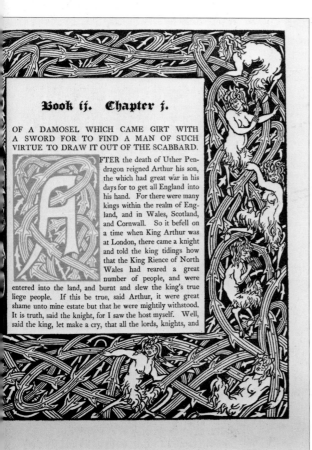

Charles Ricketts's page (*above*) from the Vale Press edition of Drayton's *Nimphidia* (1896) exhibits the grace and comparative simplicity of line characteristic of his style. His original approach to the design of initial letters is seen in his O here; entwined with knotted stems supporting a pansy motif, often seen in 16th-century initials, the simple circle of the letter pierces each leaf, the veining of which is repeated in the leaves of the border.

The initial A, one of a set drawn by Aubrey Beardsley for his edition of Malory's *Morte D'Arthur* (1893), repeats the thorny stems of the border to dramatic effect, making this page one of the most striking in the book. The letter shape, which retains something of Morris's Gothicism, is less elongated than others by Beardsley but nevertheless belongs to his distinctive art nouveau style.

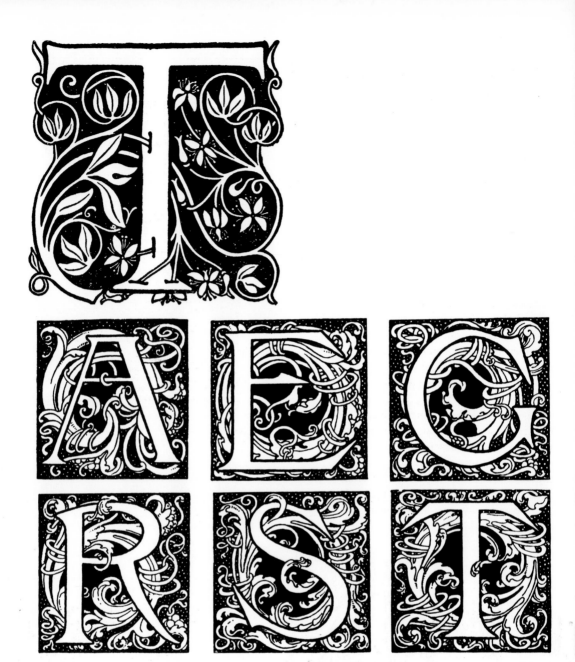

English private presses of the early 20th century continued the movement, initiated by Morris, towards the establishment of higher standards in book design. Large initial letters (*top*) created by Lucien Pissarro for his Eragny Press and shown in the 1914 special issue of *The Studio* are subtly coloured in delicate pink or green, combining the pure lines of Roman letterforms with simple, Renaissance-style flower and leaf decorations, which, like the designs of Morris or Ricketts, contribute to harmoniously effective pages. Meanwhile, other less celebrated artists had entered *The Studio*'s competitions for initial designs in the art nouveau mode, popularized by the magazine's reproduction in the Nineties of current continental letter styles. Some private presses, including the Chiswick Press, reflected fashionable trends among their long-established designs: the initial letters (*above*) of a Miss Watts, only one of many now forgotten women artists working at this period, appeared in their

catalogue.

The concept of the 'Book Beautiful', formulated by T.J. Cobden-Sanderson at the turn of the century, encouraged the adoption of 'simplicity' as the ideal in book production during succeeding decades. The effect on decorated letters is seen in the designs of Eric Gill, who during the Twenties and Thirties engraved many initials and several alphabets for type, in a style relying chiefly upon the extension of letters in disciplined floriated decorations, which enhanced rather than obscured their forms. The 'and' (*below*) from *The Four Gospels* (1931) shows his skill in placing pictures within or adjacent to his flourished letters. Other contemporary designers subscribed to the same ideal: simple lines and restrained decoration in an F (*right*), by a student at the influential Central School of Arts and Crafts in London, fulfilled both aesthetic and typographic requirements. Engraving, calligraphy and type design continued to be guided by a philosophy of restraint until recent times; the miniature alphabet (*below right*) by Reynolds Stone effectively places simple wood-engraved pictures with unpretentious Roman letters.

FROM fairest creatures we desire increase,
That thereby beauties *Rose* might neuer die,
But as the riper should by time decease,
His tender heire might beare his memory:
But thou contracted to thine owne bright eyes,
Feed'st thy lights flame with selfe substantiall fewell,
Making a famine where aboundance lies,
Thy selfe thy foe, to thy sweet selfe too cruell:
Thou that art now the worlds fresh ornament,
And only herauld to the gaudy spring,
Within thine owne bud buriest thy content,
And tender chorle makst wast in niggarding:
   Pitty the world, or else this glutton be,
   To eate the worlds due, by the graue and thee.

WHEN fortie Winters shall beseige thy brow,
And digge deep trenches in thy beauties field,
Thy youthes proud liuery so gaz'd on now,
Wil be a totter'd weed of smal worth held:
Then being askt, where all thy beautie lies,
Where all the treasure of thy lusty daies;
To say within thine owne deepe sunken eyes,
Were an all-eating shame, and thriftlesse praise.
How much more praise deseru'd thy beauties vse,
If thou couldst answere this faire child of mine
Shall sum my count, and make my old excuse
Prouing his beautie by succession thine.
   This were to be new made when thou art ould,
   And see thy blood warme when thou feel'st it could.

IT CAME TO PASS IN THOSE DAYS, THAT THERE WENT OUT A DECREE FROM CÆSAR AUGUSTUS, THAT ALL THE WORLD SHOULD BE TAXED. (AND THIS TAXING WAS FIRST

ERSTER AKT
ERSTE SZENE

SAXONIS GRAMMATICI
HISTORIÆ LIBER TERTIUS

HORVENDILLUS ET FENGO,
QVORUM PATER GERVEN
DILLUS, JUTORUM PRAE
FECTUS EXTITERAT EIDEM
A RORICO IN JUTIÆ PRAE
SIDIUM SUBROGANTUR.
AT HORVENDILLUS,TRIEN
NIO TYRANNIDE GESTA,
PER SUMMAM RERUM GLO
RIAM PIRATICAE INCU
BUERAT, CUM REX NOR
VAGIAE COLLERUS, OPE
RUM EJUS AC FAMAE MAG
NITUDINEM AEMULATUS
DECORUM SIBI FORE EXIS
TIMAVIT, SI TAM LATE
PATENTEM PIRATAE FUL
GOREM SUPERIOR ARMIS
OBSCURARE QVIVISSET.

Cujus classem varia fretum na-
vigatione scrutatus offendit.
Insula erat medio sita pelago,
quam piratae collatis utrin-
quesecus navigiis obtinebant.
Invitabat duces jucunda litto-
rum species; hortabatur exterior
locorum amoenitas interiora
nemorum verna perspicere lus-
tratisque saltibus secretam syl-
varum indaginem pererrare.Ubi
forte Collerum Horvendillum-
que invicem sine arbitris ob-
vios incessus reddidit. Tunc
Horvendillus prior regem per-

DIE TRAGISCHE GESCHICHTE VON
HELSINGŒR EINE TERRASSE VOR DEM SCHLOSSE.

Bernardo   Wer da?
Francisco   Nein, ihr steht mir rede:
    Halt! wer seid ihr?
Bern. Lang lebe der könig!
Franc. Bernardo?
Bern. Er.
Franc. Ihr kommt gewissenhaft auf eure stunde.
Bern. Schlag zwölf. Pack dich zu bett, Francisco.
Franc. Dank für die ablösung! 's ist bitter kalt,
    Und ich bin kränklich.
Bern. War eure wache ruhig?
Franc. Alles mausestill.
Bern. Schön, gute nacht!
    Wenn ihr auf meine wachtgefährten stoßt,
    Horatio und Marcellus, heißt sie eilen.

      Horatio und Marcellus treten auf.

contari nisus, quo pugnae genere decernere libeat, praestantissimum affirmans, quod pau-
cissimorum viribus ederetur. Duellum siquidem ad capessendam fortitudinis palmam omni
certaminis genere efficacius fore, quod propria virtute subnixum, alienae manus opem
excluderet. Tam fortem juvenis sententiam admirans Collerus, cum mihi, inquit, pugnae
delectum permiseris, maxime utendum judico, quae tumultuationis expers duorum ope-
ram capit. Sane et audacior et victoriae promptior aestimatur. In hoc communis nobis
sententia est, hoc ultro judicio convenimus. At quoniam exitus in dubio manet, invicem
humanitati deferendum est, nec adeo ingeniis indulgendum, ut extrema negligantur officia.
Odium in animis est; adsit tamen pietas, quae rigori demum opportuna succedat. Nam
etsi mentium nos discrimina separant, naturae tamen jura conciliant. Horum quippe con-
sortio jungimur, quantuscunque animos livor dissociet. Haec itaque pietatis nobis conditio
sit, ut victum victor inferiis prosequatur. His enim suprema humanitatis officia inesse
constat, quae nemo pius abhorruit. Utraque acies id munus, rigore deposito, concorditer

4

Dramatic use of a decorated initial, placed to form part of the illustration to the opening of Shakespeare's *Hamlet*, appears in the page (*above*) from an edition produced at the Cranach Press, Weimar, in 1929. The project, abandoned at the outbreak of the Great War, then resumed in the early Twenties, involved collaboration between the calligrapher and type-designer Edward Johnston, the artist-engravers Eric Gill and Edward Gordon Craig, and the typographer J.H. Mason, all of whom had been enlisted by Count Harry Kessler in the early days of his press.

HAMLET PRINZEN VON DÆNEMARK

Franc. Ich denk, ich höre sie. - He! halt! wer da?
Hor. Freund dieses bodens.
Mar. Und des königs lehnsmann.
Fran. Habt gute nacht!
Mar. So tretet ab, kam'rad.
    Wer hat euch abgelöst?
Fran. Bernardo steht auf posten.
    Nochmals gut nacht!
Mar. Holla, Bernardo!
Bern. Sagt, ist Horatio hier?
Hor. Ein stück von ihm.
Bern. Grüß gott, Horatio! grüß gott, Marcellus.
Hor. Nun, ging das ding auch heute wieder um?
Bern. Die wacht war ruhig, wie Francisco sagt.
Mar. Horatio glaubt an nichts, nennt hirngespinst
    Das fürchterliche schreckbild, das wir sahn.
    Und darum hab ich selbst ihn hergebracht,
    Damit der augenschein ihn überzeuge
    Und seinen zweifel tilge. Mag er dann,
    Wo's wiederkehrt, mit dem gespenste reden.
Hor. Pah, pah! Es wird nicht kommen!
Bern. Setzt euch denn,
    Und lasst uns nochmals euer ohr bestürmen,
    Das so verschanzt ist gegen den bericht,
    Von dem, was wir gesehn.
Hor. Gut, sitzen wir,
    Und laßt Bernardo, was er weiß, erzählen.

ERSTER AKT
ERSTE SZENE

LE CINQVIESME LI
VRE DES HISTOI
RES TRAGIQVES.
LE SUCCEZ & EVE
NEMENT DESQVEL
LES EST POUR LA
PLUS PART RE
CUEILLY DES CHO
SES ADVENUES DE
NOSTRE TEMPS
ET LE RESTE DES HISTOIRES ANCIENNES. LE TOUT FAICT ILLUSTRÉ ET MIS
EN ORDRE, PAR FRANÇOIS DE BELLEFOREST COMINGEOIS. A LYON PAR
BENOIST RIGAUD MDLXXXI · AVEC QVELLE RUSE AMLETH, QVI DEPUIS
FUT ROY DE DANNEMARCH, VENGEA LA MORT DE SON PÈRE HORWENDILLE,
OCCIS PAR FENGON SON FRÈRE, ETAUTRE OCCURENCE DE SON HISTOIRE.
Quoy que j'eusse deliberé des le commencement de ce mien oeuvre de ne m'esloigner, tant
peu soit, des histoires de nostre temps, y ayant assez de sujets pleins de succez tragiques, si
est-ce que partie pour ne pouvoir en discourir sans chatouiller plusieurs ausquels je ne vou-
droy desplaire, partie aussi que l'argument que j'ay en main m'a semblé digne d'estre offert à
la noblesse Françoise, pour les grandes, et gaillardes occurrences qui y sont deduites, j'ay un
peu esgaré mon cours de ce siecle, et sortant de France et pays voisins, suis allé visiter l'histoire Danoise, afin qu'elle puisse servir et d'exemple de vertu, et de contentement aux nostres,

5

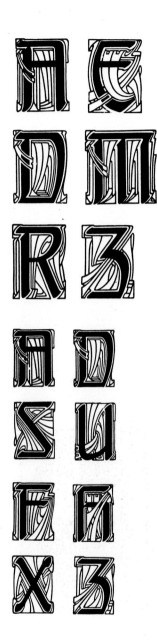

An admirer of Morris and an active patron of the arts, Kessler was also involved
with the German review *Pan*, to which the *Jugendstil* designers Otto Eckmann and
Peter Behrens contributed drawings for initials and alphabets. Eckmann's letter O
with a design of swans (*left*), popular motifs in engraved head- and tail-pieces,
appeared in 1896; the angular letters with abstract decorations, of Behrens (*right*), are
more obviously Germanic in conception.

Individual creativity, uninhibited by typographic demands, is freely expressed in the alphabet 'Sassa', drawn by the Swiss artist Imre Reiner in 1939. His use of line in conjunction with deceptively simple patterns of dots or squares, and occasionally solid infilling, gives his letters a lively vigour lacking in many modern designs. Indication of the construction of each letter, at the joins between uprights and curves, and the balance between thick and thin strokes, are executed with impressive simplicity.

An awareness of the three-dimensional quality of letters (*top right*), indicated by the use of fine lines shadowing the solid shape of each character, gives the alphabet 'Baynard Claudia' a subtle dignity. Designed by Barnett Freedman in 1935, the fluid edges of the letter exploit the block shape without ignoring the needs of typography. A return to symbolism and cipher appears in the 1964 'Alphabet Mystérieux' by Roman Gieslewicz of Paris (*below right*); some traditional components, some contemporary, are juxtaposed with skill to create letter collages.

94

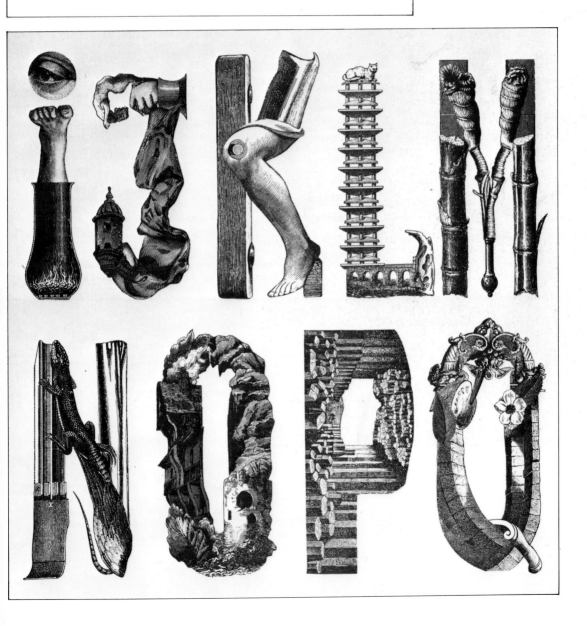

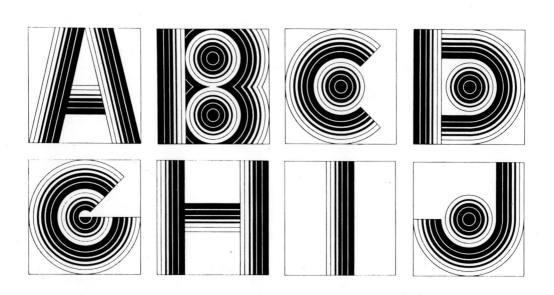

Modern styling, functional as well as decorative, characterizes two French alphabets of the Sixties. 'Calypso' (*top*) by Roger Excoffon, described in the publication *Lettera* as 'a novelty of charm and elegance', combines shadows and curves to give a three-dimensional, mobile effect. 'Or' (*centre*) revives the shape and movement of art deco styles in an uncluttered, bold design, suitable for contemporary display purposes. Such letters are, however, less personal in conception than those appearing in the *Seven Secret Alphabets* of Anthony Earnshaw, published in 1972. Here letters composed of pictorial elements, some, like the E and F (*above*), recalling earlier alphabet designs, are used, often wittily, to challenge the preconceptions of the observer. The individuality of the graphic artist, drawing upon traditions and contemporary experience, is expressed, as in the past, in the creation of letters.